The Town That Died Laughing

A Vintage West Reprint

The Story of the Mine: As Illustrated by the
Great Comstock Lode of Nevada
by Charles Howard Shinn, 1896

Eureka and its Resources
by Lambert Molinelli, 1879

Report of Explorations Across the Great Basin . . . in 1859
By Captain James H. Simpson, 1876

An Editor on the Comstock Lode
by Wells Drury, 1936

Frémont: Explorer for a Restless Nation
by Ferol Egan, 1977

Sand in a Whirlwind: The Paiute Indian War of 1860
by Ferol Egan, 1972

Silver Kings . . . Lords of the Nevada
Comstock Lode
by Oscar Lewis, 1947

The Town That Died Laughing: The
Story of Austin, Nevada
by Oscar Lewis, 1955

The Town That Died Laughing

THE STORY OF AUSTIN, NEVADA,
RAMBUNCTIOUS EARLY-DAY MINING CAMP,
AND OF ITS RENOWNED NEWSPAPER,
The Reese River Reveille

b y
OSCAR LEWIS

New Foreword by
Kenneth N. Owens

RENO:UNIVERSITY OF NEVADA PRESS:1986

Vintage West Series Editor
Robert E. Blesse

The Town That Died Laughing: The Story of Austin, Nevada, Rambunctious Early-Day Mining Camp, and of Its Renowned Newspaper, The Reese River Reveille, by Oscar Lewis, was originally published in 1955 by Little, Brown & Company of Boston and Toronto. The present volume reproduces the original edition except for the following changes: the front matter has been modified to reflect the new publisher, and a foreword to the new edition, by Kenneth N. Owens, has been added. The cover art is from an original watercolor by Dave Comstock.

Library of Congress Cataloging-in-Publication Data

Lewis, Oscar, 1893–
    The town that died laughing.

    (A Vintage West reprint)
    Reprint. Originally published: Boston : Little, Brown, 1955.
    1. Austin (Nev.)—History.   2. Reese River reveille (Austin, Nev.)—History.   I. Title.   II. Series.
    F849.A9L4   1986   979.3'33   86-7101
    ISBN 0-87417-109-1 (pbk. : alk. paper)

The paper used in this book meets the requirements of American National Standard for Information Sciences— Permanence of Paper for Printed Library Materials, ANSI Z39.48-1984. The binding is sewn for strength and durability.

University of Nevada Press, Reno, Nevada 89557 USA
© Oscar Lewis 1986. All rights reserved
Cover design by Dave Comstock
Printed in the United States of America

Foreword to the New Edition

For a brief few seasons during the 1860s, the people of Austin believed that their town, the self-proclaimed capital of the Reese River mining district, might become the Queen City of central Nevada. Looking at silver ledges that assayed richer than the Comstock Lode, Austin's promoters felt confident that a prosperous future was assured for their newly minted mining metropolis. But fate, clad in the starched white collars and oxford grey suits of New York investors, determined otherwise; the district's ore was simply not profitable enough to overcome the extreme isolation and lack of natural amenities in the Reese River country. Austin's great dreams soon began to wither away. Quickly built, the town entered a slow cycle of decline, its ultimate demise delayed by a spirit of local boosterism that long survived any reason for confidence.

The evidence of Austin's quick rise to fame and lingering descent toward obscurity was preserved in the pages of the *Reese River Reveille,* a newspaper that gained the one kind of distinction most remarkable in a landscape of sagebrush, bare mountainsides, scarce water, and empty spaces—it endured while others failed and disappeared. In time the *Reveille* became the oldest newspaper in the state with a continuous record of publication. Founded in May of 1863, the paper had outlasted three generations of editors and owners and was still appearing on a weekly schedule when, in the 1950s, it gained the attention of Oscar Lewis, a historical writer in search of fresh material.

As Lewis discovered, the *Reveille* could claim a good deal more than historical venerability. A lively journal of mining-camp life during Austin's boom years, this paper had acquired a habit of being humorous, and it carried into later years a tradition of wry backcountry wit that became a staple stock in Nevada's editorial trade. While the supply of news often ran short, the *Reveille* editors did their best to fill out their columns by adding a modicum of entertainment to the chronicle of local events. A key no doubt to the paper's ability to persist, this custom of editorial waggery appealed to Lewis. From it he fashioned the substance of *The Town That Died Laughing,* a book that conveyed something of Austin's history and the distinctive humor of its newspaper. By design not a work of scholarly scope, this volume was intended to put before a general audience a sense of the place, the spirit of the times, and the character of the people who had once paraded through the pages of the *Reese River Reveille.* It was meant to entertain by telling the story of the town and its newspaper, emphasizing the exercises in hilarity that distinguished the *Reveille* from its many early-day competitors. And if readers could also gain some insight into the broader trends of Nevada's social and economic development, so much the better.

Originally published in 1955, *The Town That Died Laughing* added to Oscar Lewis's reputation as an author of popular western history. The book appeared at a peak time in his career. A San Franciscan, born in 1893, Lewis had entered the writing profession before the First World War as a freelancer doing children's stories. After wartime service in the ambulance corps, he returned to San Francisco and became closely identified with the Bay City's developing literary scene.

Among other interests, he served for many years as executive secretary of the Book Club of California, an organization that published some of his earliest ventures into historical writing. Not until the 1930s did Lewis begin to concentrate on historical subjects, but he then quickly won acclaim as a highly adept practitioner in that particular literary form, history for the nonspecialist and general reader. His first great success was *The Big Four* (1938), an account of the founders of the Central Pacific–Southern Pacific Railroad that clearly showed Lewis's talent for shaping the materials of history into a treatment with wide appeal. As a companion piece he published in 1947 *The Silver Kings,* an entertaining study of the big four of Comstock Lode fame that signalled the author's developing interest in Nevada subjects. Among subsequent works, his *Sagebrush Casinos* (1953) gave coverage to one more popular aspect of Nevada's cultural life.[1]

The Town That Died Laughing has different concerns than most of Mr. Lewis's historical works. Not a story of eminent western capitalists, silver kings, or railroad barons, it relates the activities of ordinary people and tells of commonplace events. But definitely this is no humdrum account. In style and substance, it typifies a kind of western history that discovers in the record of the past a treasure trove of the quaint and picturesque.

---

1. For further information on Oscar Lewis and his writings, consult David Graham, "A Check List of the Published Works of Oscar Lewis," with a foreword by David Magee, Book Club of California *Quarterly Newsletter* (Spring 1975). An appreciation of his contributions to San Francisco's literary life appears in Kevin Starr, "The World of Oscar Lewis," *California History,* 58 (Fall 1984): 320–24.

Like other works of this type, *The Town That Died Laughing* commemorates the West's unique characters and peculiar doings, and it gives special attention to the whimsical vagaries and magnified conceits that lurk on the borders of conventional western experience. Lewis's volume, to be brief, celebrates the outlandish. It sets before us a magnified view of the eccentric and bizarre happenings so often nested among everyday events. And in the process, Mr. Lewis has depicted in classic form a countrified version of western regional identity, evoking a sense of self-contained, isolated small-town life that is clearly different and separate from metropolitan culture. The people who lingered in Austin, he shows us, were neither city slickers nor the naive rusticates of urban myth.

The modern reader, coming to this volume more than thirty years after its original publication, may be a mite skeptical of its claims both as humor and as history. In outline, that reader can be assured, Oscar Lewis has his history straight, though of course he did not set down the last word on Austin and the Reese River district.[2] As for humor, a subjective judgment is required. The editors of the *Reese River Reveille,* especially

2. Two M.A. theses at the University of Nevada add solid detail to the story: Buster King, "History of Lander County" (1954), and Rodney Smith, "Austin, Nevada, 1862–1881" (1963). The overall importance of Austin and the Reese River district is admirably set forth in Russell R. Elliott's *History of Nevada* (1973), the preeminent modern account of the state's development. Another book on the subject is *Austin and the Reese River Mining District: Nevada's Forgotten Frontier,* by Donald R. Abbe (1985). In addition, an excellent description of the Reese River district's railroad history fills a chapter in Gilbert H. Kneiss, *Bonanza Railroads* (4th ed., 1954).

the estimable Fred Hart who preserved for posterity the proceedings of the Sazerac Lying Club, showed occasional flashes of comedic genius. As jokesters, however, they achieved no consistent standard of rib-splitting wit; they pose no challenge to Mark Twain's title as champion storyteller of the West's Gilded Age. From the newspaper's pages Mr. Lewis has gleaned an assortment of homespun drolleries that show another type of humor: a broadly ironic, self-deprecating, even mocking outlook on life that could tolerate disaster perhaps better than it might endure some immense success. True to the Austin environment, the *Reveille* specialized in what we might call nowadays downscale merriment, putting in print small jests and items of passing amusement for its readership. Thus we can find in *The Town That Died Laughing* a chronicle of local foibles and follies, a homestyle caricature of folks who were otherwise not likely to attract much notice.

Modern sensibilities must also expect to encounter in this book the evidence of widespread nineteenth-century attitudes that, by our standards, connote ethnic and racial bigotry and sexist bias. The *Reveille's* editors did not hesitate to use the stock literary stereotypes of their time for humorous effect. Gossipy and shrewish women make an appearance here; so do lazy Indian beggars and bizarre Chinese speaking a crude pidgin lingo. But readers will find nothing vicious in these pages. If some sketches are brushed with a shade of derision, they are marked also with a customary attitude of tolerance and genial appreciation for the diversity of the West's peoples. Austin's newspapermen seem to have held firmly one tenet quoted by Mr. Lewis: "Human nature is the same the world over."

In this reprint edition, *The Town That Died Laughing* gives us a fuller understanding of the ordinary people who rushed to Nevada during the pioneer era. The volume, in ways perhaps not fully anticipated by its author, opens to view a rich pocket of social history that might otherwise remain secreted away in yellowed newspaper files, seen only by a few earnest researchers. Because Oscar Lewis retrieved the story of Austin and its newspaper from near oblivion, we can now add to our appreciation for the hardiness of those folks who came seeking their fortune in Nevada during the silver mining boom, and for the amiable spirit they could show in the face of long-term adversity. Readers will be pleased to know that the *Reese River Reveille* today still flourishes, though the paper now makes its home in Tonopah rather than Austin. And as for Oscar Lewis, it is a pleasure to report that he is alive and well in San Francisco, and at age 94 still writing.

Kenneth N. Owens
March 1986

Foreword

LIFE in the early mining towns and camps of the west was, by and large, no bed of roses, for living conditions were primitive in the extreme, the work hard and its rewards problematical, and the facilities for recreation — save for the ever-present bars and gaming-tables — conspicuous mainly by their absence. But whatever their shortcomings might have been in other directions, the residents of these raw and isolated communities were a hearty and self-reliant lot, well inured both by temperament and experience to make the best of any situation in which they might find themselves. Because nearly all the amusements available in longer established places were lacking, they proceeded to improvise their own, finding an outlet for their abundant energies — and release from the tedium of otherwise drab and toilsome lives — by all manner of expedients: impromptu games and horseplay, the spinning of tall tales about the evening stoves or camp-fires, even on occasion dances, songfests, prize fights, amateur theatricals, and other more or less formal types of entertainment.

The western frontiersman was catholic in his tastes, and he welcomed whatever might offer itself in the way of diversion — provided only that it afforded him an opportunity to laugh. For humor — the broader the better — was the quality he prized above all others; it was at once his anodyne and his safety valve, and whoever or whatever could stir him to full-chested guffaws he took to his heart.

This was a fact well known to the editors of mining-town newspapers — at any rate, to the more discerning of them — and the consequence was that the purveying of news was ever a matter of secondary importance, their primary function being, as they saw it, to provide entertainment for their amusement-starved readers. Thus they filled their columns with all sorts of items designed to produce a chuckle: humorous anecdotes, hoaxes, satire, brief sketches poking good-natured fun at local events or customs, or holding up to none-too-mild ridicule the foibles of their fellow townsmen.

Although this highly personal type of journalism was common to virtually all the early mining-town papers, it probably reached its pinnacle in two Nevada journals of the 1860's and 1870's: namely, the *Territorial Enterprise* at Virginia City, and the *Reese River Reveille*, published in the town of Austin in the center of the state. Of the two, the *Enterprise* is today by far the most widely remembered — partly because it was while a member of its staff that Mark Twain made his debut as a writer. But the *Reveille*, too, was once renowned throughout the west for the humor and uninhibited frankness of its reporting, and it is mainly in the hope of rescuing the little sheet from the undeserved obscurity into which it has fallen that the material on the following pages has been compiled.

One reason why that sprightly journal is all but forgotten today is that copies of its early issues are now difficult to come by. As far as is known, the only complete file, beginning with Volume I, Number 1, and continuing down to date, is in Austin itself, where the early volumes are safely stored in the office of the Lander County Treasurer, that official possessing the only fire-proof vault in the town. Considerable runs of the paper are to be found, too, at the Bancroft Library, Berkeley, California, the California State Library, Sacramento, and the Nevada State Library at Carson City — all of which the author has made use of and to the custodians of which he offers his grateful thanks for their unfailing interest and helpfulness.

Contents

The Town That Died Laughing

CHAPTER ONE

Ho! For the Reese River!

I

NEVADA'S oldest continuously published newspaper, the *Reese River Reveille,* has been serving its readers in the town of Austin for more than ninety years. While this, by western standards, makes the paper an authentic pioneer, it is not, as has sometimes been stated, the oldest in the area. Two or three other western journals have been published without a break longer than the *Reveille,* and of course numerous western towns were in existence long before there was an Austin. Obviously, then, it is not their age alone that makes the little paper and the little community memorable. Both have other claims to distinction, as will be shown.

First, as to the town itself. At no time in history has Austin been either very big or very important. It was a western mining town and, like all such towns, it shot up fast, had a brief season of prodigious growth and a somewhat longer period of activity while the pay ore of its ledges was mined and milled. This was followed by a long, slow subsidence as its rich veins of silver one by one pinched out, during which business stagnated, all but a few of its residents pulled up stakes and left, and the place took on by degrees the melancholy aspect of a ghost town.

4 The Town That Died Laughing

Although during its short-lived boom, its inhabitants —
again like those of every other western mining camp —
referred to the place grandly as a "city," there was never a
time when Austin had just claim to the title. Even in its
heyday, a period that lasted only two or three years,
the most sanguine of its boosters never claimed for it a
population of more than eight thousand, and there is
reason to believe that even that was at least a mild exaggeration.

That top figure of eight thousand — or seven thousand,
or six thousand, as the case may be — was reached during the years from 1863 to 1865. After that, a decline set
in, one which, despite occasional partial recoveries, has
continued ever since. Thus Austin's newspaper, the in-
destructible *Reveille,* which once chronicled the happenings of a community numbering into the thousands,
is today published in the weathered shell of a town with
a population of less than two hundred. Yet the paper continues to appear regularly, just as it has done for more
than nine decades, and — like the town itself — is now
looking ahead with confidence to the completion of its
first century and the beginning of a second. Nor do those
who know Austin, and the *Reveille,* have much doubt
that both ambitions will be realized.

To understand why the old-timers have so much faith
in the permanence of their town and its newspaper, it
will be helpful to tell something about their joint origins.
For those who might have trouble locating Austin (for
few maps list places of such small size), it should be stated
that it lies near the geographical center of Nevada, mid-
way between the California state line to the west and
that of Utah to the east, and — give or take a few miles

one way or the other — equidistant from the state's northern and southern boundaries. Austin's location is important, as its residents well know, for from the beginning it has had a decisive bearing on its fortunes, both good and bad.

The town lies in a steeply slanting canyon of the Toiyabes, one of the series of north-south mountain ranges that cover much of central Nevada. It is an area that saw little of the pathfinders who broke trails westward during the period from 1820 to 1840, or of the heavy migration set off by the California gold discovery of 1848. For the Argonauts, finding the steep, parched walls of the Toiyabes barring their way, swung to the north and followed the easier, though longer, course of the Humboldt River across two thirds of the territory until that erratic stream presently grew discouraged and sank from sight in the desert sands some eighty miles from the base of the Sierra.

Throughout most of the 1850's, therefore, Austin's site, and indeed the countryside for a good many miles in all directions, remained virtually unknown, being far removed from the main-traveled routes between the two coasts. Soon after the decade ended, however, two events took place that were to put an end to the region's isolation. Both were the result of a desire on the part of the Californians for speedier means of communication with the east coast, that being the place from which most of them had come and with which virtually all had business or social ties.

The first means of cutting down the time required for the exchange of messages between the two coasts was the celebrated Pony Express, a group of horsemen who, riding in relays day and night, covered the nearly two thousand miles between St. Joseph, Missouri, and Sacramento, California, in eight days. This reduced to less than half the time of passage between New York and San Francisco by the next fastest means: the side-wheel steamers that plied the waters of both coasts, with crossings at Panama or Nicaragua. Because with the Pony Express speed was the paramount consideration, and because the rugged terrain of the Toiyabes presented a less serious obstacle to its riders than to the overland stages and emigrant wagons, the horsemen, instead of swinging to the north and following the course of the Humboldt, took this much more direct route across the mountains.

Thus, when the Pony Express began operations in the spring of 1860, the spot where Austin was presently to rise was no longer remote; instead, it was on the shortest and speediest of the transcontinental travel routes. For, on making their way down out of the mountains and onto the Reese River plain, westbound riders passed through the narrow canyon the town was presently to occupy. To be sure, there was then nothing to indicate that in a matter of two or three years a large and extremely lively settlement was to spring up there. The riders picked their way down the steep-walled canyon, intent only on reaching Jacob's Station, some seven miles from its mouth, where they would transfer their mail bags to fresh mounts and push on westward.

During much of the following year, 1861, a new and still faster means of communication was being rushed to completion, and again its route passed through the Toiyabe Range and close to the site of the future town. Stringing the wires of the Overland Telegraph was completed in late October, and the Pony Express, having served its purpose for a little more than a year and a half, found its usefulness nearing an end. It continued in operation, however, for several months longer, and before it passed out of existence it played an indirect but decisive part in a discovery that was to draw thousands into the sterile plains and mountains of central Nevada.

How all this came about can be briefly told. In May of 1862, an ex-Pony Express Rider, William Talcott, while searching for some horses that had strayed away from Jacob's Station, entered the canyon by which the Pony Express trail wound upward into the Toiyabe Range. While on this quest, Talcott, who, like most westerners of his day, kept an eye alert for likely quartz formations, spied an outcropping of greenish-colored rock that stirred his interest. Because it bore a resemblance to certain silver-bearing ores he had seen on the Comstock — which since 1859 had been a center of feverish mining activity — he gathered up a few samples and sent them to Virginia City to be assayed. This, however, was not done with unseemly haste; consequently, several months passed before the results of the assay, which were highly encouraging, became known. Meantime, not waiting to learn what the analysis might reveal, Talcott and three friends, James and Wash Jacobs, and a man named O'Neill, staked out a claim in the canyon, which they named Pony Ledge, presumably in honor of the straying animals that had been responsible for its discovery.

Shortly thereafter, one of the three locators, O'Neill, returned to his ranch in the Washoe Valley, near the base of the Sierra. He carried with him some specimens of quartz from the ledge and one day showed them to an acquaintance, a Hollander named Vanderbosch. The other, who was en route to the Comstock, thought the rock looked promising; he accordingly took along several samples and had them examined by a Virginia City assayer. The result, while by no means unprecedented, was encouraging enough to cause him to gather a small party of prospectors and with them set out on the long trek eastward to Pony Ledge. On their arrival the group made a more detailed survey of the canyon and located several other claims. One of these, which they called Oregon Ledge, had a narrow but likely-looking vein of quartz, and specimens of it, too, were sent back to the Virginia City assay office. This time the findings were sensational. The samples proved to be so rich in free silver that, it was said, when a half dollar was pressed against the surface of the pieces the coin's imprint was left on them.

When the result of this assay became known on the Comstock, it stirred up what one observer, J. Ross Browne, termed "the most intense excitement" in Virginia City and the adjacent towns.

What if the veins were narrow? [continued this writer] nobody wanted a very wide vein when a narrow one yielded six or seven thousand dollars to the ton. The Comstock was prodigiously big and wide, but it looked poor in comparison to this. The assays were made in the latter part of December. Immediately the news spread — it flew on the wings of the wind, north, south, east, and west. Then came the great rush of January, 1863. . . .

Browne, a widely-read journalist of the day, gave this picture of the excitement that gripped the entire west coast and of the stampede that presently got under way:

Ho, then, for the Reese River! Have you a gold mine? Sell out and go to Reese! Have you a copper mine? Throw it away and go to Reese! Do you own drygoods? Pack them up for Reese! Are you the proprietor of lots in the City of Oakland, California? Give them to your worst enemy and go to Reese! Are you merchant, broker, doctor, lawyer, or mule-driver? Buckle up your blankets and off with you to Reese, for there is the land of glittering bullion, there lies the pay-streak!

So many made haste to follow this advice that during the early months of 1863 first scores and then hundreds arrived daily at the cold, six thousand-foot-high new bonanza. The newcomers swarmed over the steep, frozen sides of Pony Canyon and its environs and staked out thousands of claims, meantime living in tents, using sagebrush and bunch-grass for fuel and, for food, slaughtering the animals on which they had come.

Among the first to arrive was a Southerner named David E. Buel, who is credited with having christened the new camp Austin in memory of the town in his native Texas. Buel, who was long a leader in the affairs of the camp, had, before falling victim to the mining fever, been in charge of the Klamath Indian Reservation in California, where he had been, in the words of an acquaintance, "that rarest work of God that I know of — an honest Indian Agent."

The influx continued throughout the winter and spring, with tents and sod shanties covering an ever widening area of the canyonsides, and with shelter of any kind against the chill blasts of the wind so much in demand that the owner of a sheep corral did a brisk business selling (for fifty cents a night, in advance) sleeping space within the enclosure. Meantime, the claim-holders, each convinced that his small plot of frozen ground concealed a fortune, kept vigilant watch over his property to ward off possible trespassers.

No man [wrote Browne, with what was probably only a mild exaggeration] could safely undertake to sleep under the lee of a quartz-boulder, in consequence of that claim being guarded by a prior occupant armed with a six-shooter. . . . It was a luxury to sit all night by a stove, or stand against a post behind a six-foot tent. I have heard of men who contrived to get through the coldest part of the season by sleeping when the sun was warm, and running up and down Lander Hill all night; and another man who staved off the pangs of hunger by lying on his back for an hour or so at meal-times with a quartz-boulder on his stomach.

With the coming of spring, trains of freight wagons began to rumble in from the west, each piled high with food and whisky, clothing, gambling paraphernalia, mining tools, and lumber. By midsummer of 1863, the population of the area — which a year earlier had been deserted save for occasional roving bands of Shoshone and Piute Indians — was said to be in excess of four thousand. These were mainly congregated in two camps, both complete with stores, bars, hotels, and clusters of cabins and tents. One was Austin itself, an elongated settlement occupying the narrow trough of the ravine, and the other was Clifton, on the floor of the Reese River plain at the entrance to Pony Canyon.

Inevitably, a keen rivalry developed between these two camps, for each aspired to become the trading and recreation center of the booming new district. At first the advantage was all on the side of Clifton. For although it was more than a mile distant from the cluster of mining claims, its site was level and the wagons bearing goods for its merchants could unload at the doors of the stores, whereas only a trail, too steep and narrow for any vehicle to negotiate, led upward to the canyon's floor where Austin was located.

The resourceful Austinites, however, presently hit on a means of overcoming that handicap. Whereas Clifton property-owners were setting high prices on building sites in their camp, its competitor offered merchants free land for their stores provided they joined in a community enterprise: that of building a road connecting their town with the floor of the plain. The result was that what one early visitor termed "a magnificent grade" was laid out and finished in record time. When it was completed, Clifton found itself no longer the terminus of the numerous stages and wagon trains carrying passengers and freight to the new camps; instead, it became little more than a way-station on the road to Austin. Clifton's decline, hence, was even more rapid than its rise had been. A traveler, passing that way a scant two years after its first streets had been laid out, thus described the scene:

All that remains of it now is a broad street flanked by the wrecks of many frame shanties, whose lights are fled and whose garlands must be dead, for they are nowhere seen, unless the everlasting bunches of sage that variegate the scene should be regarded in that metaphorical point of view.

In May of 1863, however, the two towns were still of approximately the same size, and both were growing by leaps and bounds. A comparison made during that month showed Clifton slightly ahead, with an estimated five hundred residents to its rival's four hundred fifty, with eight saloons to Austin's five, and with its main thoroughfare having the distinction of a name — it was called Montgomery Street after San Francisco's fashionable promenade — whereas Austin's steep and winding roadway was still nameless. Both places, though, were alike in one respect, for each boasted an equal number of establishments which the compiler listed guardedly as "2 —— houses."

The complete catalogue of Austin's business concessions, made up, as the man who compiled it pridefully pointed out, "when the town was not yet six months old," was as follows:

Two hotels, 2 stores, 5 saloons (and 2 building); 1 billiard table; 2 meat markets; 1 bakery; 2 stationery stores (and 2 building); 1 variety store; 3 laundries; [the aforesaid] 2 —— houses; 1 livery stable; 2 lawyers; 4 notaries; Wells, Fargo & Company's Express; Turner's Express; Telegraph office; 1 barber shop; 1 tailor shop; 1 sign painter; 4 carpenters; 4 stone masons; 2 adobe yards; 4 handsome gardens; 1 boot and shoe store; 1 dairy, and 1 printing office.

II

THE last-named establishment is important, for even at
that early date the town boasted its own newspaper,
and it was in the columns of its second issue, that of May
23, 1863, that the above compilation was published. This
journal was — and is — of course, the *Reese River Reveille*
which today, as it has done for ninety-two years, continues to keep residents of Austin and its environs informed
on local happenings, with occasional half-grudging references to less important events transpiring in other parts of
the world.

Volume I, Number 1 of the *Reveille* appeared on May
16, 1863, less than four months after the first makeshift
cabins were thrown up in Pony Canyon. Its founder
was a printer named William C. Phillips who had arrived
with the first wave of emigrants, bringing with him the
equipment needed to set up in business as printer and
publisher: a small hand-press, a limited assortment of type,
and a few reams of paper. The diminutive, six-column,
four-page journal, with a page-size measuring 11½ by 15½
inches, appeared first as a weekly. In its initial number,
Owner-Editor Phillips announced that in politics the paper would be staunchly Republican, an unwavering supporter of the Union forces in the war then raging, and that
it would at all times devote its best efforts to furthering
the interests, not only of Austin, but of such other Reese
River mining communities as might be founded.

Evidently these objectives found prompt favor, for
despite the little paper's by no means niggardly cost —
its price was fifty cents a copy, $24 a year — it was widely

read, and from the first, advertisements were numerous, occupying more than two thirds of the space in its narrow, crowded columns. Moreover, on June 6, after only five issues, it became a semiweekly, appearing on Wednesday and Saturday mornings. At the same time, its price was reduced, subscriptions becoming sixteen dollars a year by mail or express, and single copies twenty-five cents. Meantime, the volume of advertising — mainly announcements of the steadily growing number of business establishments, together with notices of the incorporation of numerous mining and milling companies — increased to the point where, in order to prevent the news from being crowded out entirely, single-page inserts, called "Supplements", bearing the overflow were issued with almost every number.

Because during that period, and for several years thereafter, space was chronically tight, both local and outside news, the latter received over the wires of the Overland Telegraph, was rigidly compressed, with few stories occupying more than an inch or two of type. Many of these terse paragraphs, however, shed revealing light on what manner of life was lived in the fast-growing camp. Thus, its seventh number, that of June 13, contained this item:

Small change — that is, already coined small gold or silver — is in great demand here. Business is very much retarded for the want of it. Gentlemen coming out should not bring a twenty-piece if they can help it — bring small change and get "a premium."

During June, Austin's first death was reported, the victim being a thirty-three-year-old native of Tennessee who succumbed to "lung fever," a common, and usually fatal, malady in all western mining towns. A week later came the announcement of the first birth, "a fine, fat boy, the personal property of Mr. and Mrs. W. M. Middleton, of upper Austin."

The editor's use here of the term "upper Austin" is significant, for a few issues earlier he had issued this warning:

QUIT IT. — Several of us new-comers have been in the habit of calling the upper part of the town Houston. That is *non est* — the name is null and void and there is no such town. It's all Austin; so understood and so accepted in law and equity. Remember this.

Throughout the summer and fall of 1863, the influx, both from the east and west, continued unabated. With "people arriving by the scores in every manner of conveyance" and "hotels and restaurants crowded to the utmost inconvenience," the scene was one of round-the-clock bustle and confusion. On November 11, the *Reveille* commented:

There seems to be no decrease in the number of immense freight wagons which are daily seen in the streets. . . . Last Saturday about noon the attention of many persons was attracted by seeing the road across the valley almost covered with teams. The sun was shining brightly and the whole scene reminded one forcibly of a '49 emigrant train wending its way to the new-found El Dorado. Last Thursday Buel & Terrill paid out $6,000 for freight, and the bills for the remainder of the town must have amounted to at least $20,000.

The fifteen-cent-per-pound rate fixed by the wagon-train operators for carrying goods from Sacramento to Austin, and the correspondingly high passenger fares charged by the stage lines, apparently had no effect on the heavy volume of traffic flowing across the Sierra and over the rutted and dusty trails through the sagebrush. On October 7 the paper reported that during the course of the one-hundred-eighty-mile journey from Virginia City to Austin one traveler had counted 274 freight teams, all headed eastward, as well as nineteen passenger wagons, 3 pack trains, 69 horsemen, and 31 who were trudging along on foot.

At the same time [continued this account], two lines of stages from Virginia City were booked from six to seven days ahead; and parties in Virginia [City] who never intended to come to Austin made a good speculation by booking and selling their chances, at a good advance, to persons who were afraid the claims would all be located before they could get to the scene. . . .

With virtually all these newcomers intent only on locating one of the rich silver ledges, merchants and other businessmen were hard put to it to get help to conduct their booming enterprises. In August, the *Reveille* complained that the upbuilding of the town was seriously retarded by a lack of laborers of all sorts, despite the high wages being offered. Two months later, however, that difficulty seems to have been overcome, for in its issue of October 10 the paper reported a building boom in full swing as the inhabitants made haste to provide shelter against the storms and freezing temperatures of the coming winter. "A gentleman [it stated], in strolling up the canyon the other day, estimated the number of buildings in the course of erection at not less than three hundred, ranging in size from the 7 x 9 cabin to the stately 25 x 75 store."

One result of this belated building boom was to send the cost of construction materials to astronomical heights.

Clear sugar pine [reported the *Reveille* on November 14] is now selling at $500 per thousand feet; common inch lumber is in demand at $400, and siding at $300 — shingles sell at $25 and $30 per thousand, and shakes at $10. Common inch doors are worth $10, and windows (8 x 10) are in demand at $5.50 — other sizes at $8 and $10. Lumber is far from being a drug on the market, and we have heard of several large sales being made, and the money paid, while it was still on the road.

Prices of other commodities tended to change rapidly, depending on how big a supply was on hand.

The market here [the paper stated on November 7] is exceedingly fluctuating, as an article that is very scarce one day may be plenty the next. At present the articles mentioned below rate as follows: Flour, $20 to $22; bacon, 40 to 45 cents; beans, 20 cents; potatoes, 15 to 18 cents; butter, 65 cents; lard, 45 cents; sugar, crushed, 45 cents; ditto, New Orleans, 35 cents; coffee, 65 cents; apples, 20 to 25 cents; molasses, per gallon, $3; wood, per cord, $15.

Food for animals was usually very high, with hay sometimes bringing as much as eight dollars per hundred pounds, and barley was virtually unobtainable at any price. On November 7, under the heading of "Lucky," the *Reveille* printed this item:

A gent who owns a hay ranch in this vicinity offered to sell out, six months since, for $300, but was unable to find a purchaser. During the past season he has cut on his ranch, and sold, $4000 worth of hay.

Through that summer and fall, there were numerous stories of handsome profits reaped by Austin residents. Usually these were a result of sharp rises in the value of parcels of land near the center of the town, which were much in demand as sites for stores, bars, and other commercial enterprises. Typical of these is the following, which appeared on November 25:

LUCKY SPECULATION. — Two months since, Mr. William Brown of this city purchased a lot on Main Street for $900, which he sold two weeks ago for $4,000. Four hundred and fifty percent is pretty good interest. . . . Mr. Brown has shown his confidence in the future permanent prosperity of our town by investing his principal and interest again in Austin real estate.

III

THE rise of this new district and the well-advertised richness of its silver ledges, which were drawing thousands from other mining centers all over the west, were naturally viewed with alarm by the editors of journals published in those communities. The result was a rash of editorials in California and Nevada papers warning their readers against rushing off to Austin on what, they stated, might well prove a wild goose chase. The local paper took delight in reprinting such items and in appending appropriate comments. Thus, on October 21, appeared the following:

A California contemporary remarks: "Reese River will be all the rage, until some other God-forsaken place is found, when everybody will rush thither."

We had rather [retorted the *Reveille*] be in this "God-forsaken place," with our rich leads, than in those man-forsaken towns of California, where a man can't get grub. It suits us.

One of the favorite devices by which rival editors strove to discourage wholesale migrations to the new bonanza was to point out that the Reese River mines were located in a high, barren plateau where the winter snows were so deep that all communication with the outer world was frequently cut off for weeks at a time, thus exposing those foolish enough to go there to acute suffering from lack of fuel and shelter, and perhaps even to actual starvation. So numerous did these gloomy forecasts become that on November 7 the *Reveille* observed tartly:

We wish those smart editors who think the excitement about Reese River is growing "beautifully less," or that there is danger of starving during the winter, could have been in our town day before yesterday. During the whole

day Main street was so densely crowded with freight
teams just arrived, that it was in some places impossible
even for footmen to pass. The stage was delayed for an
hour endeavoring to run the blockade. A gentleman informed us that about noon he counted on the street sixty-
one freight wagons, and one pack train. As each of these
wagons carried between two and five tons, the sum total
of freight must have been immense.

An editorial in this same November 7 issue, bearing
the title, "Envy and Jealousy," chided these alarm-
spreading editors for what it termed their "narrow and
pinchbeck hearts." Two Nevada journals, the *Aurora
Times* and the *Humboldt Register,* were singled out for
special attention, principally because they had hinted that
the supposed richness of the Austin ledges was all a mi-
rage.

They are constantly reminding their dear subscribers
[the editorial concluded] of Gold Bluff, Gold Lake, and a
thousand other humbugs that have led hundreds astray on
this coast. They wouldn't say that Reese River is such a
place, not for the world, but then it is well to be on guard.
Besides, Tom Jones — everybody knows Tom — has just
returned from there, and he says he would much prefer
Lick-Skillet Gulch, and we hear of numbers of others who
intend returning soon. And then too the winters are terrible out there, Mr. Johnson having informed us that he
once passed through the canyon where Austin is now situated when the snow was fully twenty feet deep, and
there are not enough provisions on hand for one month,
and no prospect of getting any more.

Although the *Reveille* scoffed at predictions that residents of the new camp would face dire perils and privations during the coming winter, there is evidence that during the fall of 1863 the Austinites themselves looked forward to the frigid months ahead with considerable misgiving. As early as September, the paper, having stated that newcomers were still arriving, "in wagons, stages, buggies, on horseback and afoot," at the rate of from seventy-five to one hundred a day, added gloomily: "Not a solitary cuss brings his own grub; hence they only increase the chances of starvation or depopulation in the winter."

A little more than a month later, on October 17, appeared this item:

A local in a late number of the *Alta* [of San Francisco] says: "If one thinks that residents of Reese River are going to starve the coming winter, they need but to look at the directions on the thousands of packages of goods destined for that locality, as they lie piled on the Broadway Wharf every afternoon."

Send them along immediately, Mr. *Alta* [counseled the *Reveille*], for if the rush continues, as present appearances indicate it will, all the available teams in California cannot freight enough over between now and the time the snow will blockade the mountains, to begin to supply our wants.

The *Reveille's* running feud with journals published in other western mining towns was, however, not exclusively concerned with the question of whether or not residents of the new camp would survive their first winter. Virginia

City papers, and those of other Comstock towns, had from the beginning of the Reese River rush disparaged the importance of the discoveries, pointing out that the ledges, while some were admittedly rich, were extremely narrow, not to be compared with the inexhaustible bodies of ore to be found in their own mines.

In its issue for November 7, the Austin paper thus answered one such charge:

A late number of the *Gold Hill News* contains the following:

"A gentleman just in from the Reese River informs us that the ledges there which are called a foot thick are generally from one to two inches, and those called five feet will be found to be about two. What a lying age we live in."

Of the truth of the last remark [added the *Reveille*] there could be no better example than the item which precedes it.

Throughout the spring of 1864, Austin having meantime survived its first winter without undue hardship, the exchanges with other mining town editors went merrily on, as indicated by this item in the *Reveille* for February 25:

LARGE ASSAY. — "We saw a few days since a certificate of an assay by Veatch & Company, which showed about the largest yield we have ever heard of. The rock was from the Warner & Wells ledge, and the yield was $22,519." — *Reese River Reveille.*

"Can't you take some of that back . . . ? Take off $20,-000 and we'll take your word for the balance." — *Placerville News.*

Not a cent, Mr. *News,* will we "take back." The yield as reported by us was correct — $22,519 per ton — fabulous as the sum might seem to you and the rest of the outside world. If you are incredulous you can take a walk up to their shaft, and there find several hundred pounds of ore, each pound of which will pay at least three dollars, besides any amount of ore of poorer quality, which alone would astonish the natives of any other district than this.

That derogatory comment on the state of affairs in the new town did not all originate in the rival mining districts of California and Nevada is indicated by the following letter, written by a resident of the nearby settlement of Jacobsville, the former pony Express station on the floor of the valley, some seven miles to the west:

Jacobsville, June 8, 1863

Mr. Editor: How do you do, way up in Austin there? Why don't you come down into the white settlements? If you will come down and make us a visit here, I will take you around and show you some of the prettiest ladies on the Pacific Coast; then I will introduce you to some pretty gay widows also. There is the beautiful Miss J., and Miss K., then there is pretty little Miss S., with her nice curls, then there is the gold widow L. of the L. Hotel, then there is the dashing little black-eyed widow, St. C., who is going to California in a day or two — but to return again. Then if you are not satisfied, I will see that you become acquainted with some of our fine looking married women.

You fellows can brag of your rich mines and mountain fevers up at Clifton and Austin, but they are nothing to be compared with our pretty women at Jacobsville. But I want to give you a little advice if you conclude to pay us a visit; don't for goodness sake, bring Sam Langhorne, of Clifton, with you, because he comes often, yes he does. Everybody is a friend of Sam, although I am a little down on him. I don't know as he is to blame because the girls, *and widows,* like him better than they do me.

The letter was signed "Tortio, Jr.," Tortio being the name of the chief of a band of Shoshone Indians then encamped in the area. The mention of a lady-killing Clifton visitor bearing the name Sam Langhorne arouses a certain amount of curiosity, since one Samuel Langhorne Clemens was, of course, then in Nevada, having come out some two years earlier with his brother Orion, who had been appointed secretary of the territory. However, whether or not the reference in this letter was to Mark Twain — and whether he had a hand in its writing — must at this late date be left to conjecture.

IV

ALL during its turbulent, fast-growing early months, Austin was, as its newspaper frequently pointed out, making rapid strides toward shunting off the crudities of mining camp life and embracing the refinements of

civilization. Thus, in mid-June of 1863, less than a month
after the paper was founded, it proudly announced the
organization of a seven-piece band, and a week later
called the attention of music-loving residents to the fact
that the Austin Glee Club was in process of formation.
Then, on July 22, appeared this item:

A school has been opened up town — under a pine-
bough shelter. Fast — ain't we! A school, printing office,
numerous large frame and stone buildings, innumerable
cabins and shanties, three mills going up and two more to
arrive in a few days, and all done since January!

Through that first summer and fall, virtually every issue heralded further evidences of progress. In August, it
was announced that a public-spirited citizen had contributed the land for a school and that a fund was being
raised to erect a building on the site that would properly
house the town's fifty or sixty children, who were then receiving instruction beneath the woefully inadequate pine-
bough shelter. Later that month, an editorial pointed out
that the commercial life of the town was badly hampered
by the lack of a bank, and before the year was out it carried word that two local men, John Paxton and A. Thorn-
ton, had founded the Bank of Austin, with a capital stock
of $400,000, which, in addition to doing a general banking
business, was prepared to purchase bullion. In early November came the announcement of the arrival of uniforms
for the local band, which then boasted eleven members,
and on November 25 the editor advised his readers to
"grease up your boots, put on your store clothes and 'biled

shirts' and attend Austin's first Grand Ball, scheduled to be held in the International Hotel."

The International, which today is still doing business at the old stand, was then — as now — the social center of the town. Its history is not only a long but an eventful one. First built at Virginia City in the spring of 1860, the structure was dismantled three years later to make room for a more pretentious hotel about to be put up on the same site. The rush to the Reese River being then at its height, the lumber was loaded on wagons, hauled over one hundred eighty miles of desert to Pony Canyon and there reassembled. Although it at first had only a temporary roof of cloth, the transplanted International did a booming business throughout that first summer and fall. In October, the *Reveille,* in carrying news that the hotel's owners were arranging to provide their patrons with more adequate protection against the snows of the coming winter, added: "It has done business to the amount of at least $100,000 under a canvas roof and certainly deserves something better in the future."

With a school, a bank, and a hotel — to say nothing of an assortment of stores, bars, and gaming-rooms — the time was ripe for other improvements, including those designed to promote the spiritual welfare of the miners. These, too, were promptly forthcoming. On July 29, the *Reveille* announced the founding of the first Sunday school, its sponsor being one Reuel C. Gridley, a local grocer who, as we shall see, was presently to focus nation-wide attention on the town. A month later, the Reverend Adam Bland, Presiding Elder of the Methodist Church for the Nevada District, arrived and announced that he would conduct services, the first in the Reese River area, on the following Sunday morning. "We are informed," stated the *Reveille,* "that it is his intention to provide for the spiritual necessities of this community by establishing a minister among us at an early day," adding pointedly: "There is a good field for one here, certainly."

This item in the issue for November 11 makes it clear that plans were then afoot for the founding of a second church:

> LIBERAL. — The proprietors of Walton's addition . . . yesterday presented a lot 100 foot square on the corner of Paul and Pine streets to J. H. Root and H. D. Chambers, to hold in trust for Bishop Talbot, of the Episcopal Church. Such liberality is creditable, and we trust that the day is not far distant when a fine church will be erected upon this lot. We understand that the Bishop stated when he passed through here a few days since, that he would soon send a minister to this section.

During that same month, the editor, abandoning for once his policy of praising all things connected with the best and most progressive of western mining towns, published his description of "An Austin Bath," describing it as "Two inches of cold water, a piece of brown soap, a towel about half the size of the *Reveille* — and a dollar and a half."

Comment of that sort was, however, far from common. As far as Austin was concerned, the emphasis throughout was on Progress, with a capital P. Rarely did an issue appear without at least one paragraph heralding some new civic advancement: the removal of the Lander

County courthouse from Jacobsville into its handsome new quarters "on upper Main Street, near the Surveyor's office"; word that the receipts of the local office of the Overland Telegraph had topped twenty-five hundred dollars during October 1863, making it the company's third most profitable office on the entire west coast; finally, as the year ended, came this news of the successful outcome of a campaign the paper had been waging for months:

The Postal Department has at length been satisfactorily convinced of the fact that there is such a place as Austin, and we take pleasure in informing our readers that the difficulties of the Clifton Hill are to be overcome by the establishment of a Post Office here. . . .

Through the editor's rose-tinted glasses all things pertaining to Austin, and the Reese River in general, looked favorable. It is not surprising therefore to learn that even the peculiarities of its climate (which half-frozen newcomers had recently been terming "atrocious") presently came in for its share of praise, a paragraph in the issue of October 14 stating:

A correspondent has discovered the reason why this is a fast country. He ascribes a portion of it to the great quantity of electricity in the atmosphere. He says his blankets, when he shakes them at night, light him to bed with their electric light, and the hair of his bedfellow serves him as a beacon from afar, showing a striking resemblance to the head of Perseus above him. The vividness of this electric power has often been remarked in this section, as extraordinary both in power and brightness, and it is not impossible that it exerts a powerful influence on the human system, assisting materially in the creation of that reckless impetuosity which is driving the whole community forward to the accumulation of wealth.

The *Reveille's* editor did, however, admit — half grudgingly, it would seem — that the town's six-thousand-foot elevation had one minor drawback: at that high altitude, stated he, the pressure of the atmosphere was so light that wearers of false teeth had difficulty keeping their upper plates in position.

During the first several months, much stress was laid on the fact that the camp was a model of tranquillity, its residents uniformly peaceful and law-abiding, with the trouble-making element so numerous and bothersome in most newly founded western communities happily absent. Life here, the editor maintained, was as serene and untroubled as in the old-established towns of the east, with every man respecting the rights and property of his fellows and crime and violence virtually unknown.

It was an alluring picture the *Reveille* painted during these early weeks; unfortunately, though, it could not be long sustained. For here the rich new strikes, like those elsewhere, attracted not only honest miners but, close on their heels, a horde of gamblers, sharpers, and loose women, all intent on gathering in their share of the easy profits. The result was that the editor was presently not only reporting frequent acts of violence but urging that steps be taken to bring the situation under control before it got entirely out of hand. "Let Austin be an exception to the rule of rowdiness and lawlessness in mining camps," he counseled, "and the town will receive its reward in increased and permanent prosperity."

Unhappily, this advice failed to stem the tide, and through the summer and fall of 1863. the columns of local news were liberally sprinkled with stories of evil-doing. Thus, in the issue of November 29, the editor wrote gloomily:

BLOODY. — We give accounts today of two murders and one shooting affray (probably fatal) which have taken place in the vicinity within the last few days. Our town had heretofore been surprisingly peaceable, but if bloody lawlessness is not soon nipped in the bud the consequences to the whole country will be severely injurious.

The *Reveille* believed that the widespread habit of carrying firearms was the cause of much of the bloodshed, and in the same issue as the above appeared a sober editorial pointing out the dangers of that custom:

IMPROPER USE OF FIRE-ARMS. — One of the crying evils which beset a community where the population is hastily congregated from all parts of the continent, is the universal practice of carrying, and the too frequent use of, deadly weapons. A week seldom passes during which we do not hear of weapons being drawn for trivial provocation, and too frequently with fatal effect. . . .

Too frequently, innocent parties suffer by this wanton violation of law and order. While we ignore the code duello, except in extreme cases, we think it much better that when ruffians use "villainous saltpeter," they go out and quietly exchange shots according to the book. So long as ruffians are permitted to make walking arsenals of themselves, peaceable citizens are compelled to carry weapons in self-defense. Our civil authorities should at once take a decided step in the matter and whenever a rowdy or loafer is caught with an assassin's tool on him, give him the extreme penalty of the law. . . .

Another practice the peace-lvoing editor deplored was that of certain miners who, after an evening in one or another of the town's numerous bars, gave vent to their exuberance by stepping outside and taking pot-shots at whatever targets presented themselves. These nightly fusillades grew so frequent as to cause the editor to write querulously: "If people must fire their pieces why do they not go to the hills where the room is ample and no person is in danger of losing life or limb?"

Thievery, too, was common throughout the winter of 1863-1864, with numerous reports not only of the pilfering of articles ranging from boots, shoes, and other wearing apparel, to the rifling of the merchants' strong-boxes and the robbery of citizens abroad late at night on the unlighted streets. Such holdups presently became so frequent that, in the issue of February 9, the *Reveille* remarked that "It would be a blessing to the community if some of these night-hawks could be introduced to a bullet while engaged in their illegal avocations."

The high prices prevailing during that first winter made the pilfering of foodstuffs a highly lucrative operation and the tactics of the thieves correspondingly bold, as witness this brief item on November 18, 1863:

FLOUR THIEF. — Night before last the occupants of a tent in the rear of Hallowell & Company's store went to bed leaving five sacks of flour piled up at the door within a few feet of them, but in the morning they were astonished to find that the whole pile had left for parts unknown.

It presently reached a point where thievery and other misdeeds became so recurrent that when a full twenty-four hours passed without any new crimes being reported, the editor was moved to comment on the abnormality. Thus, on June 19, 1864, appeared this mildly apologetic item:

QUIET. — Everybody was remarkably quiet last night [a Saturday] in the city; not a drunk or disorderly case was to be seen on the streets. Consequently we have no murders or robberies to report this morning.

The town's prostitutes were a frequent source of trouble during the first several years, all of which was grist to the editorial mill. On June 16, 1864, appeared this more or less typical paragraph:

ATTEMPT TO KILL. — We learn that a young lady (?), a resident of the adobe house kept by Lizzie Moore, was terribly beaten and choked last Tuesday night by some person — name unknown. No arrests have yet been made.

On the day after Christmas of that same year came this more detailed story:

ROW IN A BAWDY HOUSE. — We are called upon to chronicle another disgraceful affair which occurred in the house of one Belle Wilder, yesterday morning about four o'clock. A courtesans' ball was being held, and at the hour above named, the fun grew fast and furious and a row was determined upon by some of the participants. The lights were extinguished and a new style of music was introduced, the instruments consisting of revolvers and derringers. Several shots were fired, one taking effect in the leg of a man named Joseph Randal. We are informed that the bone is severely fractured and that amputation may be necessary.

Like most mining-town journalists, the *Reveille's* editor was never averse to doing a bit of editorializing in his news stories, and in this instance he added a moralizing paragraph.

This [he stated] will be paying dearly for a night's fun. Randal is employed in the capacity of private policeman in our city and is well known. This should be a warning to honest men against frequenting houses of this ilk. A man named Charles Moore has been arrested and charged with committing the deed, and will be examined tomorrow, when further developments will probably be made public.

This episode had a tragic aftermath, for some days later the paper reported that the fellow had died, a victim of blood poisoning. What punishment, if any, was meted out to the assailant must be left to conjecture, for no further reference to the matter appeared in the *Reveille.*

Some three months later, on March 31, 1865, the

town's booming tenderloin houses were again in the news, this time as a result of gunfire by one of the lady inmates:

SHOOTING. — On Monday evening, a fair courtesan of Pine Street and her lover quarreled; "true love never did run smooth"; and while exchanging compliments in language more forcible than polite, accompanied by a rapid and effective exchange of tumblers, pitchers and other convenient furniture — implements of warfare known to that fraternity and sisterhood — a passer (he had better passed), attracted by the tumult, entered the portals of love's adobe, and like the valiant knight of La Mancha, rushed to the rescue. A lull in the battle gave Madam an opportunity to draw a pistol from beneath the cushion of a sofa, and she would undoutedly have given her *cher amie* a satisfactory dose of cold lead had not her Don Quixote grasped the muzzle of the weapon and took the charge through his hand and into his leg below the knee, making a quite severe though not serious wound. Latest reports are "all quiet on Pine Street."

V

ALTHOUGH from the beginning it was the policy of the paper to deplore serious breaches of peace or decorum, its editor nonetheless recognized that life in a raw frontier town had aspects that, while they might be considered scandalous in older established communities, were here regarded as normal behavior, to be treated as routine news and reported with a sort of humorous tolerance. One such story appeared on February 23, 1864:

PRIZE FIGHT BY MOONLIGHT. — Austin has been the theater of one of those muscular exhibitions. Night before last an Irishman and an Englishman, between whom there was an old dispute, met in a saloon near the corner of Main and Cedar streets. They quarreled and finally agreed to settle their difficulties according to the laws of the ring. They thereupon immediately adjourned to the street. Mac Waterhouse was selected by the Englishman as his second, and George Loney by the Irishman, and after these preliminaries had been gone through with, the mauling commenced about twelve o'clock. Twenty-one rounds were fought and for a time the battle was very hotly contested, both giving and receiving very hard knocks and showing no signs of yielding. But Johnny Bull's endurance was too much for Irish grit, and victory was decided in favor of the Englishman. It is claimed, however, that the result was entirely owing to the instructions Mac gave his man during the twenty-first round; that is, to feint with his left, take one step back, and give an uppercut with his right. This direction was followed and gained the fight. Both men were severely punished. A large crowd witnessed the contest, many being present in dishabille, not having had time to dress themselves when they jumped out of bed to see what was going on. We are making fine progress ·in "muscular Christianity." A prize fight in our most public thoroughfare. Who can beat it?

Although excessive drinking on the part of many of the inhabitants was from time to time deplored by the paper, the editor recognized that the town's barrooms were the chief — and indeed almost the only — centers of conviviality for the town's predominantly male population. Consequently, the tavern-owners were looked on as substantial members of the community, provided only that they conducted their establishments in a seemly manner. Indicative of this attitude is the following, which appeared on April 19, 1864:

NEW SALOON. — John L. Hale, late of Clifton, has fitted up and opened one of the neatest saloons in Austin, near the corner of Main and Virginia streets. The floor is finely carpeted, the bar handsomely fitted up, and well-furnished, comfortable easy chairs, tables, newspapers, and a superb lunch, with polite and handsome bartenders, are among the attractions of the Merchants' Exchange. We prophesy that Hale will get what he deserves to have, a good share of the public patronage, and that the Merchants' Exchange will be no misnomer but a fair exchange of good money for a good drink.

Of Austin's abundant bars, virtually all of which were also gaming rooms, Samuel Bowles, editor of the *Springfield* (Mass.) *Republican,* who passed through on the way to the west coast in June 1865, reported that, while "not a tree, nor a flower, nor a grass plot does the whole town boast . . . one of the finest specimens of feminine physical beauty and grace presides over a lager beer saloon." He added that "gambling riots openly in a very large area of every drinking shop — miners risking to this chance at night the proceeds of the scarcely less doubtful chance of the day. . . ."

One advertisement in the columns of the *Reveille* in-

terested Bowles so much that he copied it out and published it for the enlightenment of his subscribers at home:

Mammoth Lager Beer Saloon, in the basement, corner
Main and Virginia streets, Austin, Nevada. Choice liquors,
wines, lager beer, and cigars, served by pretty girls, who
understand their business and attend to it. Votaries of
Bacchus, Gambrinus, Venus or Cupid can spend an evening agreeably at the Mammoth Saloon.

Both inquisitive and classical [the New Englander com-
ments] we went in search of this bower of the senses; and
we found a cellar, whitewashed and sawdusted; two fid-
dles and a clarionet in one corner; a bar of liquors glaring
in another; and a fat, coarse Jew girl proved the sole em-
bodiment and representative of all the proclaimed gods
and goddesses. We blushingly apologized, and retired
with our faces to Mistress Venus, Cupid, etc., as guests retire from mortal monarchs — lest our pockets should be
picked; and we shall take our mythology out of the dic-
tionaries hereafter.

By the time the town and its newspaper had entered
their second year, one of the editor's main concerns was
to point out that Austin had outgrown its rowdy, helter-
skelter youth, and to urge its residents to behave accordingly. Population was still increasing and substantial
buildings of adobe, brick, and native sandstone were re-
placing the temporary wooden structures, all indicating,
according to the *Reveille*, that this was no fly-by-night
mining camp but a city destined to become the trading
and supply center for a rich new mining and agricultural

region. "The town is spreading out upon the hillsides," the editor stated on March 3, 1864, "and has about reached the extreme limits up and down the canyon. Before next August we expect to see the sides of Austin and Lander hills [the steep canyonsides to the north and south] well covered with houses."

Firmly convinced that the town's future was assured, Editor Phillips frequently pointed out the desirabilty of undertaking civic improvements designed to give the place a physical appearance in keeping with its importance. In particular he deplored the town's barren, unkempt appearance, and on May 28, 1864, he suggested this means of beautifying the cottages and cabins clinging to the canyonsides:

We cannot forbear urging our friends to spend a little portion of their leisure in adding to the adornment of their homes. A few vines here and there, a few rose bushes, and just a little taste to set them out, will relieve the plainness of many an otherwise attractive dwelling. The Reese River bluejays and all the other birds will kindly lend their little aid to the undertaking by giving you the best music they have in their little throats.

A few days later, on June 2, he proposed another needed civic betterment. This time he wrote with considerable feeling, his subject being:

DOGS. — Had we the power to hitch another injunction to the half score of commandments, we would add: "Thou shall keep no worthless cur dog." Go where you may, you are sure to stumble over half a gross of good-for-nothing members of the canine family. Now, in these war times, when we have heavy taxes, heavy duties, and heavy expenses all around, we think a moderate tax of about five hundred dollars per head upon curs would be welcome by the nation at large. A measure of this kind would, aside from its propriety, stamp the originator with the impress of true statesmanship. . . .

This blast was soon followed by yet another step in his one-man clean-up campaign, this time directed at the Main Street merchants:

It is a matter of reproach to our city, particularly to those whose fault it is, that we have such obstructed, dirty sidewalks. In many places there has never been anything done to make them passable, and whenever there is a rain they are extremely bad. We hope the City Council will at once take the matter in hand, and require property owners to make respectable sidewalks past their premises.

Austin's future was much in the thoughts of the *Reveille's* editor all during this period and at frequent intervals he advised his fellow townsmen on their civic responsibilities. "Now that it is an established fact that our section is to become prosperous and permanent," he wrote on June 7, 1864, "and the task of developing our resources left to ourselves, it is proper that we take a good look at the work before us and set about our business with a will."

He went on to point out that while the Reese River mines were then, and were likely to remain for many years, the chief industry of the region, it was a mistake to look on its mineral resources as its only source of wealth. "It is not out of place," he added, "to remind those who may desire to come to Reese, and who may not feel disposed to enter into the laborious business of silver mining, that our country possesses within herself, aside from her inexhaustible metals, the essential elements of prosperity."

Looking ahead, he saw prosperous farms covering the floor of the Reese River valley, and the rise of Austin not only as the area's chief trading and distributing point, but as a manufacturing center. "The time is not far distant," he continued, "when our butter and cheese will be of home manufacture, our fruit, pork and poultry home raised, and manufacturies of all kinds in full blast, thereby supplying our wants quicker and cheaper than we now get them by the tedious and expensive conveyance by way of the deserts." His long and sanguine forecast of Austin's bright future ended with this advice to his fellow townsmen: "Let us have no fears that we are not laying the foundations of a large and flourishing city."

VI

THAT the *Reveille's* original owner, and his successors, were convinced that the town would have a long and prosperous life is clear from the fact that, as funds became available, a series of improvements were made in the paper and its plant.

Changes of ownership occurred from time to time. Its founder and first editor, William C. Phillips, having launched the weekly in mid-May of 1863 and converted it into a semiweekly a few issues later, remained in charge for only five months, when illness caused him to retire. Accordingly, on September 30, a brief note on the editorial page announced that he was leaving for the east and that during his absence the journal's "entire business and editorial management" would be entrusted to O. L. C. and J. D. Fairchild.

The Fairchilds, who were to supervise the operation of the paper for the next seven or eight years, during the first few months as lessors and thereafter as owners, were printers, one of whom, O. L. C., had been associated with Phillips since the first issue. The new managers promptly instituted a number of changes, the first of which was announced soon after they took charge; that is, the removal of the plant to larger and more convenient quarters.

This, a two-story stone structure, "on Pine Street, nearly opposite the Austin Restaurant," was a source of pride to the Fairchilds who, in the issue of October 7, boasted that their "little country paper" was the "only one in the Territory which has a house of its own — a fine, comfortable stone house at that." Pressroom, composing room, and editorial sanctum occupied the ground floor of the newly completed building and the floor above was rented to the County Recorder, the seat of Lander County having recently been transferred from Jacobsville to Austin. In its issue of November 25, the paper thus saluted its new neighbor:

The County Recorder's office has been removed to the second story of the *Reveille* building. Being under our immediate supervision, we hope to be able soon to enlighten the benighted fellows attached to the Recorder's corps, and "learn" them the difference between their woodpile and "our'n," and our hatchet from "ther'n." We all belong to the "pen is mightier than the sword" division, however, and it is to be hoped that we can live together amicably. If they behave themselves and don't shake too much dust down on our table all will be well.

From this time on, the successive editors followed the policy of sharing with their readers, usually in a humorous vein, the trials and rewards of publishing a newspaper in an isolated mining community, thereby firmly establishing a tradition of personal journalism that has been maintained throughout the ninety-odd years of its existence. Thus, during its early months, under the heading of "Poetry," it confided that "We have several poetical effusions on hand, some of which are very good, others distinguishable from prose only in that every line begins with a capital. Our limited space prevents us from publishing, at present, any of it." In the very next issue, however, room was somehow found for the doggerel of one of the numerous rhymsters among its readers, and thereafter there was rarely a number that did not contain one or more examples of home-grown verse.

Because the wires of the transcontinental telegraph line passed over the Toiyabe Mountains at a point close to Austin, the *Reveille* had from its founding a feature rare in western mining-town journals of the day: a column of late news from the eastern states and abroad. During the first several winters, however, heavy snowfall and violent storms often put the wires out of commission. In consequence, notices appeared from time to time explaining the lack of such dispatches, of which the following, dated April 7, 1864, is typical:

The storms toward the east have so interfered with the telegraph that we are without our usual dispatches. We hope that Grant, Sherman, Napoleon, and the Danes will take notice and not do anything exciting or desperate until the wires are in order, so we can hear the news.

Soon after moving the paper into its new quarters, the Fairchilds made two additions to the editorial staff. Adair Wilson, "late one of the editors of the Virginia City *Union*," was installed as editor, with Myron Angel as his assistant. The latter, long a prominent figure in newspaper circles on the coast, became a sort of roving correspondent, visiting the numerous camps that had sprung up throughout the Reese River district and bringing back glowing accounts of their present activities and future prospects, all of which he signed "Angel."

On February 9, 1864, when he was about to set forth on another such tour, the paper issued this reassuring word to residents of the places he planned to visit:

AN ANGEL ON THE WING. — If any of our friends at Bunker, Summit, or the Santa Fe districts should happen to descry in their neighborhood a sleek looking individual, astride an old white plug, accompanied by a suspicious looking keg, and looking very hungry for beans and "feet," they needn't be afraid of him, but can show him around; he isn't a preacher — nobody but our "special" on a tour of observation.

William C. Phillips had meantime returned to Austin. He was, however, far from well and remained only long enough to sell the paper to the Fairchilds before returning east. "He took his departure yesterday [stated the *Reveille* on May 27, 1864] for the home of his friends of former days, upon the beautiful prairies of Illinois. He goes overland in a pleasant private conveyance, and we hope that the journey may be one of pleasure, and restore him to perfect health." Within six months, the paper, having in the interval published several letters from its ailing founder, carried the news of his death.

In the meantime, in the issue for November 25, 1863, came the announcement of a further advance: henceforth, the paper would be a triweekly, appearing on Tuesday, Thursday, and Saturday mornings, and with its cost to subscribers reduced to one dollar and a half per month by mail or carrier. Readers were assured that each of the three weekly numbers would contain "as full and detailed telegraphic reports direct from the East as are to be found in the San Francisco papers," and that such reports would reach residents of Austin and other Reese River communities "at least two days earlier than they are received at present through the San Francisco and Virginia City papers."

The town being then at the height of its boom, advertising continued to be offered in such volume that even after the change to a triweekly it could not all be crowded into the regular four-page issues. Consequently, frequent "Supplements" continued to be added to take care of the overflow. With such business thus plentiful, the publishers presently inserted this notice on the editorial page: "Persons finding their cards or advertisements left out of the

Reveille will please remember that they have failed to settle up for a month or two past. We have no room for 'deadheads' at present."

By way of bringing home to the public the fact that, as the editors contended, the paper was avidly read by every living thing in the area, this item appeared on November 11, 1863:

BENEFITS OF ADVERTISING. — Some days since a gentleman living in Austin lost a valuable pocket-book near San Francisco Canyon. He advertised his loss in the *Reveille,* and a few days afterwards a coyote brought in the missing book, and left it on the snow near the owner's door.

During that fall of 1863, a recent addition to the staff of the *Territorial Enterprise* at Virginia City began attracting attention by a series of hoaxes and other wildly extravagant yarns he was contributing to its columns. One of these, a circumstantial account of a particularly gory Indian raid on settlers in the Carson Valley, had been widely reprinted all over the coast, both editors and readers accepting it as true until it was presently exposed as a hoax. On November 7, the *Reveille,* which had not been taken in by the story, paid its respects to its perpetrator in these words:

A CANARD. — Some of the papers are expressing astonishment that "Mark Twain," the local of the *Territorial Enterprise,* should perpetrate such a "sell" as "A Bloody Massacre Near Carson," a pretended account of which recently appeared in the columns of the *Enterprise.* They don't know him. We would not be surprised at *anything* done by that silly idiot.

The paper continued as a triweekly until the end of its first year. Then, with the appearance of Volume II, Number 1, came another notable advance: its change to a daily and the enlargement from its former five-column size to the full nine-column page then standard in the metropolitan journals.

The style, manner and political tone of the paper [wrote the publishers in its first issue as a daily] are so plainly set forth in this number that we deem it superfluous to multiply words on a subject so plain that anyone may understand us and our future course by merely perusing what is herein published. We need only add that we shall endeavor to keep up with the times in every respect, and print a paper equal to the demands of our young city and its extensive mining region. In enlarging the *Reveille* to its present size we are perhaps ahead of the wants of the country, but shall not fail of success if our citizens continue that liberal patronage which they have always extended to the paper.

The owners' concern that their paper's new size might prove, as they expressed it, "ahead of the wants of the country," proved to be all too well founded. For by the spring of 1864, the rush to the Reese River — which had been in full tide for many months — showed every sign that it had passed its crest. Moreover, many of the ledges, the unprecedented richness of which had drawn hordes of prospectors, speculators, and camp followers from all over the west, had pinched out after being followed only a short distance underground, while others, though they contained much greater quantities of ore, had their silver in combination with other substances that made its recovery a complicated and highly expensive process.

When these facts became generally known, the influx of newcomers tapered off and, although numerous new mining companies continued to be launched and speculation in their "feet" remained active on the exchanges at San Francisco and other coast cities, the unbridled optimism of former days gradually subsided.

All this was, of course, reflected in the fortunes of the *Reveille,* notably in the amount of its advertising. The result was that on August 2, only seven weeks after it had become a full-sized daily, it resumed its original, five-column format, becoming again what its bigger rivals at Virginia City scornfully termed a "seven by nine sheet."

Some three months later, on Saturday, November 27, this notice heralded a further change:

Hereafter [it was stated] the *Reveille* will be issued as an evening paper, the next number appearing Monday afternoon instead of on Tuesday. The change will enable us to make up our mail some twenty hours earlier than heretofore, as the stage now passes going each way about midnight.

The proprietors went on to assure the readers that no other changes were contemplated, that all the usual features and services would be maintained, and that, finally, although it was becoming an evening paper, it had no intention of changing its name from *Reveille* to *Tattoo,* as some had suggested would be more appropriate.

VII

FROM then on, evidence accumulated that the paper was sharing with the rest of the town the effects of the slack business that had followed the high-rolling days of 1863 and early 1864. In the issue of December 16 appeared a column-long notice, headed "Black List," containing the names of several scores of individuals and companies (many of the latter picturesquely named mining corporations) indebted to the *Reveille* for advertising, job printing, or other services, the amounts ranging from a few dollars to sums running well into the hundreds.

Although times continued bad throughout the winter of 1864-1865, the little daily, in its role as spokesman not only for Austin but for the entire Reese River district, continued to view the future with its confidence unshaken. The current period of retrenchment it dismissed as a passing phase, terming it nothing more than the "growing pains" that were a natural result of too-rapid expansion in the past. The highly speculative early days were, it stated, happily gone forever; with numerous mining properties of proved value just getting into production, and mills for the reduction of their ores being rushed to completion, the entire region was entering an era of stable, sustained prosperity.

In support of that theory, the paper stressed the rise in recent months of promising new mining fields at Eureka and elsewhere, proof that the mineral wealth of central Nevada was far more extensive than had theretofore been supposed. Indeed, the *Reveille* foresaw the not-distant day when the Reese River country would become the most populous and prosperous part of the future state of Nevada, and its editor looked forward to the day when Austin, as the leading city of the area, would become the logical place to locate the state capitol.

Further evidence of the unshakable confidence of the *Reveille's* proprietors in the region's future was forthcoming a few months later with the announcement that a press of the latest design, together with other modern printing appliances, had been ordered and would shortly be installed. "We have received a telegraphic dispatch from Sacramento [it stated in early April] that our new office equipment was there, en route to this place. We are assured that it is one of the finest and most complete ever started mountainward. We have not yet received the details but expect to soon. Then we will make our light shine!"

Later that month, it was announced that the editorial staff had been augmented by the addition of a "local editor," and on June 4 came word of yet another extension of its news coverage:

OUR SAN FRANCISCO DISPATCH. — Having made arrangements for a daily San Francisco dispatch, we shall hereafter treat our readers to all the news of importance transpiring in the metropolis of the Pacific or that centers there from the state of California or the countries upon the coast or the other distant parts of the world. All news transpiring there up to the hour of our going to press will appear in the columns of the *Reveille* each day.

However, despite all these evidences of the owners' confidence in Austin's future, the looked-for upturn in business stubbornly failed to materialize. Dull times, which at first had been looked on as merely a passing phase — "a necessary period of change and readjustment," the *Reveille* had hopefully commented — persisted from month to month, with many of the richest mines of the area one by one suspending operations while their employees drifted off to new districts then rising to prominence.

It was, of course, not long before the *Reveille*, along with every other business in the town, began to feel the pinch. The paper's declining revenue presently made necessary drastic cuts in its expenses. The first step in this policy of retrenchment came on February 17, 1865, when it was announced that the plant was being moved from its former rented building, the Fairchilds having, they stated, purchased "our own house" on the opposite side of the street. Making the best of the matter, the announcement read:

Our new quarters are more roomy and comfortable than the old and we derive an exquisite pleasure from knowing that at the beginning of each month we have no heavy rent bills to pay. We feel very happy in the contemplation of our new position, but we are not stuck up by the transition. In fact, we are still ready to furnish the public with our paper as usual and, it may be, with more than the ordinary amount of interesting reading matter. We are also willing to advertise at the old rates, to execute job work as neatly and expeditiously as ever, and will endeavor to deport ourselves toward the world as though it had advanced in a corresponding ratio with ourselves.

Despite the optimistic tone of the above, it was clear that times in Austin and its environs were slack indeed, with money tight and all segments of the population practising unaccustomed economies. The fact that the Lander County officials had recently been following this trend by placing printing orders with San Francisco firms instead of patronizing home industry — namely, the *Reveille's* job printing department — brought forth this spirited protest in the issue of February 20:

We know [the editorial stated] that the county is in debt, and that bitter hard times reign in the community. The narrow pages of this paper, the dearth of business advertisements, the numerous sheriff's and constable's sales, the appeals to charity by many suffering laboring families, all tell the story in language stronger than we can depict it.

The *Reveille* has done all that could be asked in making known the resources of the Reese River. No inland paper on the Pacific Coast is more generally quoted from; while it makes known to the outer world the wealth and capabilities of the country, it supplies its home readers at great expense the current and interesting news of the day. The *Reveille* compares favorably with any paper in the United States published in any town the size of Austin, and for such reasons considers itself worthy of liberal support.

Adding to its already heavy problems was the fact that just at that time a member of the staff sustained a severe personal loss, the details of which were related in the same issue:

MYSTERIOUS DISAPPEARANCE. — The gentleman who furnishes local literature for this journal begs to inform the public that a bovine quadruped of the feminine gender was abducted from her home on Saturday last, while in blissful repose near our country villa. Or in plain Saxon, some infernal, thieving scoundrel stole a cow from our wick-i-up on Turner's Ranch, and thus robbed our wife and little ones of their allowance of milk. Said cow is light red, has horns projecting forward, one of which has been bored. Anyone who will leave word at this office which will lead to the detection of the thief and recovery of the cow, or point out the fellow who stole her at a distance from which he can be covered by a double-barrel shotgun, will be paid the full price of the animal.

Although there were occasional brief periods of renewed activity, mainly due to the discovery of promising new mines in the area, Austin was never again to experience anything remotely approaching the prosperity of its initial boom. From 1865 onward, the fortunes of the town went into a slow but steady decline, one that was destined to continue down to the present.

Notwithstanding persisting hard times, however, the Fairchilds continued to get out their little daily for five years longer. Then, in the summer of 1871, a change of ownership was announced, the new publishers being Andrew Casamayou and John H. Dennis. A little more than two years later, on September 9, 1873, Dennis sold his interest to John Booth, Casamayou becoming editor. On December 12, 1875, yet another change was announced. Casamayou retired, and throughout the balance of that decade and well into the 1880's, John Booth & Company was listed on the masthead as publisher. During much of that period, the paper was edited by Fred H. Hart whose contribution to the *Reveille's* story deserves a chapter to itself.

CHAPTER TWO

The Sazerac Lying Club

I

YOUNG Fred Hart, having served his apprenticeship on various papers in California and Nevada, joined the *Reveille* in the fall of 1873, at about the time John H. Dennis withdrew and sold his interest in the property to John Booth. He was associated with the journal for approximately five years, during most of which time he occupied the post of editor. His connection with the *Reveille* — and Austin — ended in November 1878.

Austin [he wrote in the late 1870's] is a small, interior mining town, ninety miles, by a rough road, from the Central Pacific Railroad, having its communication with the outer world carried on by means of mud-wagons, called by courtesy stages; and, it can readily be conceived, a quiet place, in which anything of a startling nature in the line of news seldom transpires.

His editorial duties included about everything in a writing line that needed to be done, from "composing an advertisement about a lost dog up to heavy dissertations on leading topics." His chief responsibility, however, was that of gathering up each day enough items of local news to fill several columns on the inner pages of the little sheet.

There was no difficulty about the leaders or other editorial matter [he recalled]. A pair of sharp shears, a raid on the exchanges, and the texts from the telegraphic news daily supplied the paper, would readily furnish them; but to make up respectable local columns was a constant strain on the mental capacity and legs of the writer, and he had almost said, "on the imagination," but a strict moral training in early life, etc., caused him to confine himself strictly to the facts.

In his daily rounds in search of "Local Jottings," it was his habit to drop in at one of the town's numerous bars. This resort was The Sazerac, so named for a then popular brand of brandy; it was a favorite gathering place for a group of old-timers who, in the editor's words, "during the long winter evenings sat around the stove, smoked their pipes, fired tobacco juice at a mark on the stovepipe, and swapped lies and other reminiscences."

I had [his account goes on] long had my eye on the place as one liable at any time to pan out the text for a local, and would drop in there nearly every evening and listen to the conversation in the hope of picking up from it the hoped-for item; but the stories were generally so devoid of a semblance of truth or appearance of probability that, as a consistent journalist, whose mission and duty it was to present the public with cold, bare-faced facts, I was unable to reconcile my conscience to the "writing up" and publication of such yarns.

On one such visit, Hart listened while a regular member of the group, a man well known in the town, regaled his companions with what purported to be a description of a pile of silver bars he had once seen awaiting shipment at one of the ports on the west coast of Mexico. "His story," the editor wrote, "was an outrageous exaggeration — there could be no doubt about that; for all the silver ever produced by the famed bonanzas of the Comstock, if heaped up, would not make a pile seven miles long, forty feet high, and thirteen feet wide, and it was in the neighborhood of these figures that he placed the dimensions of the heap of silver he was describing."

This preposterous yarn did not seem to him to offer material for a local item, and he accordingly "went out of the saloon, thinking what a magnificent liar this man was, and how he had mistaken his vocation, and what a splendid journalist that elastic and towering imagination might make of him."

The next day, however, found the town in the grip of a storm, with the wind swirling down the canyon so penetratingly that few residents ventured outdoors, and news items were, in consequence "as scarce as honest savings bank presidents." The hard-pressed editor was, he added, "almost in despair about filling the local columns, and mechanically went to the door, opened it, looked out into the storm for inspiration. The street was deserted, all was bleak and blank, and I was on the point of going back into my sanctum to meditate the most painless method of death by suicide; when the narrator of the preceding evening crossed the street."

At that moment, the call for "Copy" came from the composing room, and the editor in desperation seized a pencil and dashed off the following:

ELECTED PRESIDENT. — The Sazerac Lying Club was organized last night, our esteemed, prominent, and respected fellow-citizen, Mr. George Washington Fibley, being unanimously chosen president of the organization. There was no opposing candidate; his claims and entire fitness for the honorable position being conceded by common consent of the Club.

The item duly appeared that evening and was, stated its author, read with some amusement, not only by the group at the Sazerac, but by the rest of the town. In the course of the afternoon, however, the victim of the joke appeared at the office and, brandishing his cane, angrily demanded "an apology, or a retraction, or some other foolishness," leaving only when Hart had agreed to meet his wishes.

Writing an apology [commented the journalist] is not a pleasant task for an editor. When one has said that the minister ran away with the deacon's wife, and it turns out that it was not the deacon's wife, but the deacon's wife's mother who accompanied the minister on his flight, it is rough to be compelled to apologize to the old lady on her return — not that ministers ever run away with deacons' wives' mothers, but just to suppose a case, for the sake of illustration. When you have written up a public ball, and said that "Mrs. Smithers, wife of our respected fellow-citizen, the Hon. Thomas Jefferson Smithers, who did himself and the county so much credit in the Legislature eleven years ago, was charmingly dressed in green tarletan and had her hair in curls," when the fact of the case is that she looked like the last rose of summer, and was dressed in yellow silk, and had her hair done up in a wad on the top of her head, it is mortifying to the editorial heart to take back the green tarletan and curls in the next issue of the paper. These, however, are but chips of the cross a country editor has to bear.

But he had agreed that he "would atone for the slight cast upon Mr. Fibley's fair name," and he proceeded to do so. Accordingly, the next issue of the paper bore this item:

APOLOGETIC. — An apology is due from the *Reveille* to Mr. George Washington Fibley. We said in yesterday's issue that he was elected President of the Sazerac Lying Club. This was an error; he was defeated.

Hart's account of the episode concludes with these words: "Mr. Fibley was satisfied, his ruffled feelings mollified, and from that time forward we were the best of friends."

Having thus introduced the Lying Club to his readers, the editor found that organization so fruitful a source of copy on dull days that he returned to it again and again. Possessed of lively imagination, he seemingly had no trouble conjuring up further tall tales alleged to have been told during the nightly sessions at the Sazerac. The fact that the yarns were not only relished by the local residents, but were presently being reprinted in other papers all over the west coast, is readily understandable. For their author had a nice talent for a type of frontier humor then one of the standbys of western journalism. Moreover, being himself a veteran of the California and Nevada mining camps, both his characters and the yarns

they spun had, despite the eccentricities of the one and
the exaggerations of the other, the ring of authenticity.

Certainly the regular members of the Club and the
other faithful attendants at its nightly sessions were all in
character, readily recognizable types in every west coast
mining community during the 1860's and 1870's. One
such was "Uncle John" Gibbons, stage-driver extraordinary. Gibbons, having spent some years piloting six-horse
coaches over the Sierra between Sacramento and Virginia
City before the completion of the railroad, had — like
most of his fellows — been forced off the main-traveled
routes by the advent of the iron horse. When we meet
him he is driving a "mud-wagon" between Austin and
Belmont, a now deserted town some ninety miles to the
south.

Every day of his life [wrote Hart of "Uncle John"] —
except when he is laid up with rheumatism, which periodically attacks him — he is on the box, starting at daylight in summer and completing his task in the evening;
but in winter, frequently not reaching his destination until midnight, or even daylight next morning. In summer,
over the hot alkali deserts and parched mountain ranges;
in winter, through cold and ice and snow and wind such
as constitute the almost arctic severity of that season in
the mountains, Uncle John is ever at his post, calmly ful-
filling the destiny which made him a stage-driver, and
which will keep him one until Death puts on the brakes
and he "pulls up" at the "Home Station" at the end of
his life's "route." He never leaves the box, except when
rheumatism knocks him. Then he wraps his feet in
barley sacks, gets him a cane, pulls his broad-brimmed hat

down over his eyes, takes his place at the stove, and joins the Sazerac Lying Club.

One of Uncle John's yarns — which was destined to attract attention in places far removed from the little Nevada town — is here reprinted as it originally appeared in the *Reveille:*

When it came his turn at the regularly called session of the Sazerac Lying Club last night, Uncle John Gibbons stated the circumstances that caused the detention of the Belmont and Austin stage the other day. He said that while crossing Smoky Valley, a short distance this side of the salt-marsh, he observed what he at first supposed to be a heavy bank of dark clouds descended on the valley. [A phenomenon by no means unusual in this section, and termed by the Shoshone Indians "Pogonip."] As the stage approached nearer to the object, however, he became convinced that the mass was composed of living creatures. From here we will tell the story in his own words:

"The team was gittin' kind of scary, but I held 'em level, and as I kept gittin' nearer I saw the thing warn't nothin' but a flock of sage-hen; so I jest threw the silk at the leaders, and yelled fire and brimstone to the wheelers, calk'latin' to slash the team squar' through the flock without any trouble. But, boys, thar was more sage-hen obstructin' that road than I had reckoned on; and when them thar leaders struck into them thar sage-hen they was throwed back on their ha'nches just as if they had butted clean up ag'in a stun' wall. As far's you could see there warn't nothin' but sage-hen; you could about see the top of the pile of 'em; but thar was no more estimatin' how thick it was through than estimatin' how old a hoss is by twistin' its tail. Thar I was banked up by a lot of insignificant sage-hen, and the United States mail detained in the big road by feathers — as you might remark. Wal, to make a long story short, I onhitched one of the leaders and straddled him and rode back to the station for help.

"Thar was a fellow from town doin' some prospectin' on one of the hills near the station, and when I got to the house this here prospector was sittin' by the fire, havin' come down to borrow some matches. I stated the situation in a hurry, and the hostler and the cook they saddled up some of the stage stock and got a couple of axes, intendin' to go back with me and chop a road through the sage-hen. But this here prospector he spoke up and says he:

"'See here, boys,' says he, 'don't you think we could blast 'em out quicker'n we could chop through 'em?'

"And the hostler and the cook spoke up and said they thought so, too.

"And then this here prospector he went up on the hill and got his drills and his sledges and a lot of giant-powder cartridges and some fuse, and the rest of the blastin' apparatus, and then the whole raft of us started back for the place where the stage was; and when we got thar — well I wish I may be runned over by a two-horse jerkwater if there was a sage-hen in sight as far's a man could see with a spy-glass.

"I hope you fellows is contented now you know what kept the stage late the other night."

Of the subsequent history of this tale, Hart wrote that it was reprinted in a number of papers in this country and eventually crossed the Atlantic and was picked up by a German journal, the *Karlsruher Zeitung.*

In due course of time [continued he] a German resident of Austin received from a relative in the Fatherland a copy of the paper containing the . . . curious and truthful story, and showing me the marked paragraph, explained its purport. To verify his translation I took it to a German friend, and requested him to render it into English, which he did, and as a result handed me the following:

"In Austin, Nevada, America, there is a society whose objects are competitive lying. It is under Government patronage, and the member of the Association who tells the best and most unreasonable lie is awarded a gold medal worth fifty thousand thalers. The awards are made annually by a commission appointed by the Governor of Boston, and which is in perpetual session at the seat of the National Government in New York. The lie which took the premium this year was told by Uncle John Gibbonich. He said that while riding post across the Valley of the Smoke, there arose from the earth a flock of geese so numberless that they blocked the road and shut out the light of day. And in order that the blockade might be raised, and the royal mails pass on their way, it was deemed useful to telegraph for a corps of sappers and miners from the Government barracks, who mined a tunnel through the mass of geese, and the post proceeded on its way."

To the above, Hart added a scholarly note explaining that the sage-hen is a member of the grouse family, then

numerous in central Nevada, and that it derived its name
from the fact that it feeds on the vegetation characteristic
of the semi-arid state; that is, the sagebrush. "The birds,"
he concluded, "are unknown in Germany, but in order to
reach the comprehension of his readers, the editor of the
Zeitung converted them into geese."

II

BECAUSE the newspapers of Virginia City and other
Nevada towns, as well as those in California — most
of which, like the *Reveille* itself, frequently lacked
enough real news to fill their columns — presently began
reprinting stories of the Lying Club, it was not long before that Austin institution had become known all over
the coast. The result was that a San Francisco publishing
house, Henry Keller & Company, asked Hart to compile a
book dealing with the club and its members, its text to
be made up of items clipped from the files of the paper.
This the editor was by no means disinclined to do, and
the result was that a little volume, entitled *The Sazerac
Lying Club,* made its appearance in 1878, went into a
second edition later that same year, and then — like the
town of its origin — passed almost completely from the
public eye.

In his introduction to the work, Hart wrote:

This book has been compiled and prepared in the intervals of daily editorial labor, and no claim of literary

merit is made for it. The majority of the clipped sketches have been widely copied by the press, which circumstance has had weight in causing him to believe that they possess some little merit in a humorous sense; but of that, as well as the other material herein contained . . . the reader must be the judge. This is not a "no cure, no pay" book, and booksellers are instructed, under no circumstances, to return money to persons who pronounce it a fraud. If his wishes in this matter are strictly carried into effect, the bookseller will at once proceed to bounce the dissatisfied customer, and reason with him to the fullest extent of his muscular ability. . . .

As to the scope and purpose of the work, and the nature of its contents, the author further stated:

This purports to be a book on lies and lying, but it does not treat of the lies of politicians, stock-brokers, newspaper men, authors, and others, who lie for money; neither does it touch on the untruths of scandal, mischief, or malice, but only on those lies which amuse, instruct and elevate. . . . The book contains [also] a number of sketches of odd characters in Nevada, and local narratives of life in Austin . . . which have been clipped from the files of the *Reveille* and made to do service in padding out this book to a sellable size.

The Club, by Hart's account, was a highly dignified organization and its meetings were conducted with a decorum in keeping with the seriousness of its purpose. On one occasion, he reported, on learning that the members were to assemble that evening, he made his way to the

Sazerac quite early so as not to miss any part of their deliberations.

Although it was not yet seven o'clock [he continued] the Club was already organized, Mr. G. Washington Fibley, the President, occupying his usual position in the chair. As it was the opening night of the session, after calling the roll, the President addressed a few remarks to the Club as follows: "Fellow members of the Lying Club. — I have noticed that it has of late become the custom with certain newspapers to propose for membership in this Club every scrub liar that turns up. This betrays a gross misapprehension of the objects of this noble order. As you are all aware, the objects of this Club are mental culture and mutual improvement; we do not lie for greed or gain, nor do we tolerate that class of liars who by word of mouth deceive their fellow-men for wicked or selfish ends. No, members of the Club, while we permit a range of thought extending far away into the most distant depths of the realm of the impossible, and the improbable, we do not stoop to the lie of deceit; we ask no man to place implicit belief in our lies — but if any man does so believe, he sustains no injury. There, hanging on yonder wall, is a picture of that noble man and illustrious patriot, G. Washington, Esq., in the very act of tackling the cherry tree. He could not tell a lie about who cut down that tree; but, my fellow-members, does any man here present, who possesses ordinary human reasoning, believe that if G. Washington had heard of a man telling about catching an eleven-pound trout, he wouldn't have raised him a pound or two, even if he had never seen a trout in all his born days?"

These remarks being duly applauded, the President, by virtue of his rank, was called on for the first lie. This is a synopsis of what he said, and it is in the records under the title of

OOZED INTO HIM

While on a recent journey to San Francisco, he shared a section in the sleeping car with one of the Comstock bonanza kings. The monarch occupied the upper berth, and the President of the Club the lower one. When the latter arrived in San Francisco he felt a peculiar heaviness in his body and limbs, his arms and legs especially being so weighty that he was hardly able to control their motions. He visited a prominent physician, who, after diagnosing his case, told him he displayed symptoms of metallic poisoning, and advised him to go to a Hammam, a bathing establishment . . . and get himself "retorted." He accordingly went to the institution, and took a Turkish bath; and when his pores began to open, silver oozed out of his body, like quicksilver through a rag. Altogether, he cleaned up a bar valued at $417.92 and a fraction. He says the silver must have oozed into him from the bonanza king in the berth above, that night on the sleeper.

This yarn reminded another member that once, while visiting in Cairo — "a city in Illinois" — he had admired an obelisk, which stood more than two hundred feet high, was known to the local residents as Cleopatra's Needle, and had an eye so large that "even a camel could go through." On hearing this statement the Club's oldest member got to his feet and indignantly tendered his resignation, declaring that "There ought to be a limit to all things, and a story of a needle of that size was too much even for a lying club." Moreover, would someone please enlighten him as to "who in thunder this Cleopatra was, anyway, that she required such a needle as that." President Fibley soothed the ancient's injured feelings and explained that Cleopatra "was a colored woman who nursed General George Washington when he was an infant; that he (Fibley) was well acquainted with her, they having lived in the same town in Old Virginia."

This discussion of Cleopatra's Needle prompted a third member to relate the following, which Hart termed "A Fossiliferous Lie":

He had [began the narrator] been reading that newspaper paragraph which tells that a snail from the Egyptian Desert was found to be alive after having been glued for four years to a tablet in the British Museum; but, said he, "There's nothing remarkable about that. It isn't a circumstance to an experience of mine. Once, while mining in the limestone over in White Pine, I blasted out a fossil snail, which I kept for a cabinet specimen, and one day it crawled out of the cabinet and bored itself back into the limestone where it had been embedded for thirty thousand years. . . ."

One highly loquacious member of the group was a perpetually parched individual known to his confreres as "Thirsty," whose tales were embellished with frequent digressions of a philosophical nature. Here is one example of his meandering form of delivery:

"Mr. President, you and all the members here present knows that there is a proposition on foot in this here town to plant catfish in Reese River. I don't s'pose thar's a gentleman now sittin' round this here stove that isn't acquainted with the catfish; they is not indigen-oo-us to this country, but we all knowed them in our childhood's days of innocence back yonder in the States. The history of this movement about which I make reference — to wit, the plantin' of catfish in Reese River — is about the size of this: When the railroad was built from the States out here, the people what had been out here since forty-nine began to have a hankerin' for the luxuries of their youth. It's a well-settled principle, Mr. President, that anything we was fond of in the eatin' line, when we was boys, tastes better when tasted through the vista of years than the most luxurious livin' a hash-house can afford when we have become men of the world and drained the cup of luxury down to its very dregs. I want to know if there is any whisky these days in this here country that tastes as sweet and contains as active and intoxicatin' a principle as the clear juice of the grain we used to get back home when we was jest emergin' into manhood; is thar any cider seen now-a-days as is half so sweet as we used to get it suckin' it through a straw in the days gone by? No, sir; not much!

"Well, as I was a-sayin', the people of this coast, when they was placed in easy communication with the States, commenced to hanker for the good things of their youth, and the result was a natural one, 'cordin' to the laws of supply and demand. There was a demand for certain things in this country, and the people in the States commenced a-shippin' of that class of articles to this coast over the railroad. The consequence was winter apples, ches'nuts, big oysters, eels, travelin' lecturers, catfish, and various other articles what this country don't produce of its own accord. Some fellows they brought out a lot of catfish and planted 'em in the Sacramento River, and the cats they growed and increased and multiplied the earth, so to speak, till thar was a surplus of 'em in Californy. Now when Californy has got more of a good thing than she wants herself, she sells the surplus to Nevada, at a pretty considerable figger of profit; and these fellers what was runnin' this catfish business, they advertised for sealed proposals from anybody that had any streams they wanted stocked with them kind of fish. This comin' under the eye of the enterprisin' citizens of this here town, they made up a purse and ordered a lot of the fish for plantin' in Reese River. This is the history of the case, and it remains for the members of this here Club to discuss the subjeck."

The "subjeck" was duly discussed, and at such length that it — and other fish stories — occupied the members for the balance of the evening. Even then, it was far from exhausted, and on opening the next meeting, President Fibley addressed the assemblage thus:

"Gentlemen of the Sazerac Lying Club: We had a very edifying meeting last night — one that reflected the utmost credit on not only the members engaged in the debate, but on the Club at large, and which demonstrated . . . that as liars we are unapproachable; that interest in our organization is still maintained, and that notwithstanding that there is a prospect that death may one day enter our charmed circle and carry off its brightest ornaments, we still feel that the eyes of the world are upon us, and that we have a bonden duty to perform in keeping up the standard of American lying. . . .

"The subject under discussion last night [he continued] was catching fish, catfish in particular. Gentlemen, there is nothing which affords so wide a range for the talents of the liar, which offers more opportunities for economizing on the truth as the subject of fishing. Therefore, should members decide to continue the discussion under that head, the Chair will not only not interpose no objections, but will personally see to it that members are not annoyed with interruptions from any source, either within or without the pale of this Club."

Thereupon, a newly elected member, having "squirted a stream of tobacco juice on Uncle John's rheumatic foot," arose and said:

"Mr. President, speaking about fish and other animals, don't you know thar is some animals as knows as much as a human?"

"Some humans," amended a listener, and was promptly silenced by the President.

"Yes," continued the first speaker, "some brutes knows a heap; and not only that, but they is capable of feeling attachment and affection. You all know how lovin' a dog or a horse can be to his master; but 'taint often you hear tell about an affectionate fish. Is it, Mr. President?" The Chair having replied cautiously, "Not very," the speaker launched into this reminiscence:

"Wal, when I was a boy, I once run acrost a fish that was stuck after me worse than a boy after playin' hookey. I was visitin' over at an uncle's of mine that lived about

fourteen miles from our house; and one day, when I was
down to the crick, I seed a perch in the water. It was a
awful pritty fish, with red speckles all over its back, and
as shiny as a Carson dollar [a U. S. Mint had been built
at Carson City in 1866]. I was goin' to run up to the
house for a hook and line, when it stuck its head out of
the water, and looked at me kind of knowin' like. It
didn't seem to be a bit afeared of me; and when I stuck
my finger down to'rds it, it snapped and nibbled at it jist
like you've seen a pet rooster do. I had a hunk of bread
and 'lasses in my pocket — I always used to go heeled with
bread and 'lasses in those days, just as I go heeled now
with a six-shooter, as you might observe by lookin' close
— and I broke off some crumbs, and give 'em to the
perch, and he eat 'em out of my hand as tame as a kitten.

"Then I put my hand under him, and lifted him out of
the water, and stroked him down the back, jest like you
would a dog; but he never fluttered, but lay there kind of
peaceful like, and lookin' up inter my eyes, as though he
liked that sort of business. Wal, after a while I put him
back inter the water, and went up to the house, and told
about it; and my grandmother on my mother's side, who
was stoppin' at my aunt and uncle's, said I had a gift; that
she once knowed a man who had a gift like that, who
went to the Sandwich Islands, and charmed rhinocerouses
so that they could drive 'em like horses in the king's carriage; and he'd a got rich at it, only the cannibals eat
him up. His gift was only for dumb animals, and didn't
have no effeck on cannibals.

"Wal, I used to go down to the crick every morning,
and feed that perch; and when he'd hear me a-comin',
he'd commence splashing the water for joy and gladness.

Finally, one day, my folks sent for me in a hurry to come home, and I had to take the back track and leave my fish. Gentlemen, you can imagine the affection of that fish for me when I tell you he follered me home. Yes, sir, actually traveled forty-three miles afoot to our house; and when I got up one mornin', thar he was, with a willow stuck through his gills, hangin' to the latch of the front door."

"Was he still alive?" asked a member called the Doubter.

"Certainly not," was the reply; "do you s'pose a fish could travel fifty-four miles afoot, and stand up under the strain? No, sir, he was dead; but a finer tastin' fish than that affectionate creeter was when he was fried, you never eat in your life."

III

AT ONE Club meeting, the first business taken up was an inquiry into the qualifications of two persons desiring to join the organization. This discussion ensued:

"Mr. Seccertary, be there any applications for membership?" asked the President, at the conclusion of the roll-call.

"Yes, sir," replied the Secretary; "here is two applications on my desk."

"The Seccertary will read."

"Here is one from a feller in San Francisco, who says he's a newspaper editor, and therefore duly qual- "

"Hold!" exclaimed Old Dad; "them newspaper fellers can't lie."

"I beg to differ with the gentleman," remarked the Doubter; "I was readin' of an account in a paper this mornin' relatin' to a occurrence whereby a young lady run a needle into her foot a great many years ago, and after she had got married and her children had got married and had children, that thar needle one day came out of the top of one of her grandchildren's head — a leetle bit rusted, of course, but the same identical needle. Now if that ain't a lie, I'd like to know what you call it."

"Sho'!" said Dad; "that's a common occurrence; why, back in the States I knowed a woman that swallowed a —"

"I move the previous question and call for a decision of the Chair on the newspaper man," interrupted the Doubter.

"Gentlemen," said the President, clearing his throat and winking at the barkeeper, who understood the hint, and proceeded to fix it up, with a little sour in it, "gentlemen, this here question of the admission of newspaper editors into this here Club, is one of the gravest as had ever disturbed our deliberations. It has been held by competent authority that editors can't lie. For myself I'm not prepared to speak on the subjeck; but in giving my decision on this here point, I will simply refer members to article hundred and nineteen of our constitution and by-laws, which expressly forbids and prohibits the admission of professional liars into membership in this here Club. Them's my sentiments, and the Seccertary will proceed with that there other application."

The Secretary, who had just had his "pedro" caught, arose from the table, and, holding the remaining cards up towards the Chair, said:

"I hold in my hand an application for membership from a gentleman who signs himself Honorable Ananias Truefact. He's a stranger in town, but has jest caught my pedro nevertheless, and this is him sittin' at this here table."

"Are his qualifications for membership stated in writing in his application?" queried the Chair.

"No," replied the Secretary, "but he has informed me in confidence that he was borned with an impediment in his speech which positively prevents his tellin' the truth."

The question was put on the admission of Mr. Truefact, and carried, but with one dissenting vote. That one was cast by the Doubter, who in explanation of his vote stated that he didn't "take no stock in natural but only cultivated liars."

Having been duly installed, and having complied with the rule requiring newly elected members to "set them up for the boys," the stutterer was called on for a lie, and responded as follows:

"G-g-entlem'n and M-m-mister P-p-president, I ain't m-m-much on the lie; b-b-but I'll relate a ac-c-cur-rence that t-t-took p-p-place onc't when I was a b-b-b-boy, in th' earlier and p-p-purer d-d-d-days of this here Rep-p-p-public. You may some of yer p-p-p-perhaps have n-n-n-noticed that I've got a imp-p-p-ediment in my sp-p-peech. It was in the c-c-c-city of B-b-b-bosting, and I was a g-g-g-goin' along one d-d-d-day out in the outsk-k-k-skirts, when I s-s-s-seed a b-b-b-bildin' a-f-f-fire. 'T-t-twas a tr'-m-m-m-mendous b-b-big b-b-b-bildin', m-m-mor'n t-t-two hund-d-dred f-f-feet high, and l-l-large otherw-w-ways in prop-p-portion. T-t-her' w-w-warn't n-n-n-nobody b-b-b-but me in s-s-sight, and I s-tart-t-ted t-t-ter g-g-g-give t-t-t'her al-l-larm b-b-by hol-l-lerin' f-f-fire, and —"

"And I s'pose the buildin' burned to the ground before you could get the word 'Fire' out of your mouth?" interrupted the Chair.

"T-t-that's just it," returned Ananias, "b-b-but d-d-d-does t-t-the r-r-r-rules of t-t-this Cl-l-lub p-p-p-per-m-m-mit t-th' C-c-c-chair t-t-to ant-t-ticipate a m-m-m-mem-b-b-ber's l-l-l-lie?"

One evening, it being "the time of the year that, under a city ordinance, an annual tax on dogs is collected," the town's numerous canines were under discussion by the members. Uncle John, the rheumatic stagedriver, thereupon took the floor and, having been recognized by President Fibley, delivered himself of the following:

"Dogs over here in the sagebrush knows more than dogs does in Californy, 'cause they've got a better chance to learn things and post themselves. Over to Californy a dog's time is mostly taken up fightin' the fleas, and they haint got no time to waste on their education. You've all of you lived in Californy at some time or other, and you knows how it is yourselves about fleas. I had a dog thar once, and he was about as good a dog as ever made a track, but the fleas bothered him that bad that he'd go into the river and stay thar a week at a time to git shet of them. But the fleas they didn't mind that, but used to swim off to shore and camp on the bank, and wait for that dog to come out, and then they'd bounce him ag'in, and stick to him closer than a gal to a feller that she's clean gone on.

"Finally the thing got so bad that that thar dog was actooally thinkin' of suicide. I hed a double-bar'l'd shotgun in the barn whar I used to keep the dog, and that poor animal would, every once in a while, go smelling at the muzzle of that gun, and a-feelin' of the trigger with his paw, like he was figgerin' how he could have his head at the muzzle and his paw on the trigger both at the same time. But he was a short dog — leastways he wasn't long enough to reach that fur. Finally the hostler in the stage barn took pity on that thar dog, and fixed him up a collar with a lot of long iron spikes stickin' into it, with the pints outside, and that worked two ways. The dog could scratch hisself with the spikes, and when the fleas would come lightin' down to tackle the dog, they'd strike on the spikes and stick there; and when the collar got full of fleas, the hostler he'd take 'em off one at a time, and chop their heads off with the axe, and feed 'em to his chickens."

"Is that all?" asked Old Reliable, when Uncle John had concluded.

"All! Did you expect I was goin' to say the hostler killed the chickens and fed 'em to the fleas, or the fleas ate up the dog, or any such improbable lie like that? No, sir, not much. . . ."

That the Club's members kept themselves informed on current events, and in particular on the scientific advances of that fast-moving age, is indicated by the following:

The Telegraph Company is now using the quadruplex system over the Virginia City and Salt Lake circuit, by means of which four messages may be sent simultaneously over a single wire. The wire over which this system is in use passes through Austin, and has of late given considerable trouble to the operators. They have been unable to find any break, and a close examination of the wire has failed to reveal any cause for the difficulties, which for some time past have been experienced in the transmission of messages over it.

The mystery is now solved, however. In the Sazerac Lying Club, at the last session, Old Dad interpreted the cause of the trouble. After describing the quadruplex system, he explained that the strain on the wire was increased beyond the wire's carrying capacity. He said he was out at Dry Creek the day before, and that in that vicinity the wire was just humping itself, and groaning and straining and dropping words off in chunks. He examined the wire and found a knot in it, and came to the conclusion that a quadruplex message had struck the knot and got tangled up, and stuck at that point. He tried to straighten the wire out, but a section of an account of a battle between the Turks and Russians struck him in the ear and knocked him down, and he concluded that it was not advisable to fool with the thing. He had informed the manager of the telegraph office in town, as to the cause of the difficulty, and stated to the Club that a man had already been sent out with a crowbar to pry out some of the biggest words and smooth the knot down, so that the words could pass each other.

During the several years of the Club's existence, the dissertations of its members, as faithfully reported by the *Reveille,* covered an uncommonly wide variety of topics.

At one meeting, it was suggested that it would be in keeping with the scholarly objectives of the organization to have a library.

During the discussion which arose on this point [continued the paper's account] there was considerable feeling manifested by the springing of the question as to who should act as Lie-barian, each member claiming that he possessed the peculiar qualifications necessary for that office; and the Chair, being appealed to, decided that, as the Club in itself constituted all the lie-brary required, and each member was a natural born lie-barian, further debate was unnecessary on the subject, and the Club would keep on in the old groove, relying, as before, on the newspapers and religious tracts for inspiration.

Finally, however, toward the close of 1877, reports of the Club's deliberations — which had been appearing at regular intervals for several years — disappeared permanently from the columns of the little daily. Here is the *Reveille's* own account of the circumstances that led to the momentous decision:

"Gentlemen of this here Club [stated President Fibley]: As I have stated afore, we hev most important business afore us to-night. You are goin' to be called on to deliberate the gravest question that has ever come under the consideration of this here flourishin' organization from the minnit of its commencement to date. I, as I hev said, hev rastled with the problem, but it knocks the spots off me. . . . I onc't heerd a man say that in a multitude of counselors thar is safety; and I'm goin' to submit this

here question to the whole Club, not feelin' like takin'
the responsibility of decidin' it single-handed. . . . The
Seccertary will please read this, which explains itself, and
durin' the readin' let every member sit still as a mice."

So saying, the Chair handed the Secretary an envelope,
from which that official extracted a sheet of paper, and
from it read the following:

Austin, Nevada, Nov. 20th, 1877.
To the President and Members of the Sazerac Lying
Club — Gentlemen: As you may be personally and offi-
cially aware, I have, in my capacity as editor of the *Daily
Reese River Reveille,* been divers and sundry times
called upon to record in my valuable, widely circulated,
and strictly family journal, some of the proceedings of the
Club of which you have the distinguished honor to be
President and members. This circumstance has caused
the fame of the Sazerac Lying Club to spread abroad over
this land of liberty, and even across the great waters to
the effete monarchies of the old world. . . . Yes, Mr.
President and gentlemen, your fame and renown have
spread like the exhalations of the upas tree, or a Chinese
umbrella, or a Chicago girl's feet, or a church scandal
. . . until at last it has even reached unto San Francisco.
    I am in receipt of a communication from the firm of
San Francisco publishers, requesting me to endeavor to
obtain access to the archives and records of your Club,
and to extract therefrom such matter as I, in my judgment, may select, that the Sazerac Lying Club may be
perpetuated unto our children, and our children's children, and to other generations yet unborn. My object,

therefore, in thus addressing your most honorable body, is to obtain the permission as herein set forth for the purpose above stated, and to enable me to comply with the request embodied in the preceding.

> Respectfully,
> Editor, *Reveille*

"I vote aye!" shouted the Aye-and-No member when the Secretary had concluded the reading of the above. "I want to be perpetuated to rising — may I say self-rising? — generations."

"Gentlemen," said the Chair, "this is not a matter to be decided in a minnit. We must deliberate on it, calmly, deliberately, dispassionately; without fear or favor; with charity towards all, and irrespective of age, sex, or previous condition of servitude. I would like to hear an expression of the sentiments of the Club on this here subjeck."

Mr. Thirsty spoke up and said, for his part, he didn't want to be "cremated"; that he had read in a paper recently an account of the cremation of a woman in Pennsylvania, and concluded it must hurt.

"N-n-n-not c-c-c-rem-m-ma-t-t-ted, b-b-but p-p-p-p-p-erp-p-p-pet-tuat-ted, you d-d-d-"

Before Mr. Truefact could finish the sentence, the Chair called him to order, and explained to Mr. Thirsty that he had not heard the word right — that it was perpetuation and not cremation that was under discussion.

Mr. Thirsty replied that if "the rest of 'em" could "stand it," he could.

A running discussion now ensued, in which every member of the Club took part. There was a great diversity of opinion . . . , the Doubter strenuously protesting against the granting of access to the records. He became so heated in the course of the argument that it became necessary for him to retire to the bar to recuperate his wasted energies; and Uncle John took advantage of his absence to move the previous question.

The question was put . . . and the Chair decided that the Club had resolved as with one voice to give access to its archives and records. . . . The Doubter, who returned to the stove just in time to hear the decision of the Chair, immediately tendered his resignation, which was accepted by his being fired out by unanimous consent.

Uncle John then offered a resolution that reporters should not be admitted at future sessions of the Club, and that all future records of proceedings be chucked into the stove as soon as recorded. This was unanimously adopted, as was a resolution by Old Dad, that the sessions of the Sazerac Lying Club be conducted with closed doors, *now and forever after.*

Thus, insofar as the public was concerned, ended the chronicles of Austin's Lying Club. Thereafter, no further references to the activities of that renowned organization graced the columns of the town's newspaper. Perhaps the true reason why Editor Hart drew the curtain over its deliberations was that he himself was soon to shake the dust of the little mining town from his feet.

Although his invention of the Club and his faithful services as its historian marked the high point of his career, his name continued to crop up from time to time in the annals of western journalism during the next two decades. In 1880, he became editor of Mark Twain's old paper, the *Territorial Enterprise* at Virginia City, which had long been recognized as one of the leading journals of the west coast. His tenure of that office was, however — in the words of another veteran Nevada journalist, Alf Doltem — "not only remarkably brilliant but remarkably brief." It lasted indeed only about three months. The reason for its abrupt termination was that at the time Hart became editor, one of the Comstock Bonanza Kings, James D. Fair, was running for United States senator and, during a critical stage of the campaign, Hart wrote a sizzling editorial in which he referred to Fair as "Slippery Jim," not realizing that the candidate's partner, John Mackay, was one of the owners of the paper.

"Mackay came down to the office," recalled Dolten years later, "and shaking his finger fiercely in the face of Cohen, the bookkeeper, shouted: 'Look here, what son-of-a-gun wrote all this infernal trash about my partner? I own half this cussed paper and won't have Fair abused by anyone. I've a damn good mind to take a sledge hammer and smash h—— out of the bloody press!' Hart got wind of the matter and took to the sagebrush and never came back. He strayed down to San Francisco where he was employed on the *Daily Report* and some other papers, lastly to Sacramento — nothing permanently lucrative. . . . With the passing of his old prestige came declining health and ambition, and finally the end."

Hart died at Sacramento on August 29, 1897.

CHAPTER THREE

Mining-Town Journalism

I

O NE day, while out in search of an item," wrote Editor
Fred Hart in 1878, "I asked a fellow-citizen, 'What's
the news?' 'Nothing startling,' he replied."

Reflecting on this, the other commented:

Nothing startling, indeed! That man would never do
for a newspaper reporter in a small town. Why, as he
made the remark, two dogs were preparing to sign articles for a prize-fight right in front of his store; a wagon
loaded with wood could be seen in the distance, which
was sure to pass his way during the day, if something did
not break down. Two women, whom he knew to be mortal enemies, were approaching each other on the corner
above; a doctor was hurrying across the street, and a man
who always kicks up a fuss and gets arrested when drunk
was just entering the door of a saloon a block below. If
that fellow-citizen had had the soul of a reporter . . . he
would have got out his jack-knife, picked up a chip, and,
sitting down on the first convenient dry goods box, have
whittled and waited for something startling. . . .

It was indeed because there was usually a dearth of
local news, Austin being, even in its heyday, too small a

community to provide a daily newspaper with more than a meager smattering of such items, that the files of the *Reveille* give present-day readers so revealing a picture of the manner of life lived there three quarters of a century ago. For in his unending quest for copy — almost any sort of copy as long as it would help fill his daily quota of "locals" — he was forced to put into print, and so record permanently, numerous small happenings that would have been considered too commonplace to be given space in papers published in more populous centers. Yet, it is these very trivialities that readers of today find most rewarding. For it is these, and not the accounts of occasional fires, accidents, and other items of legitimate "news," that enable one to gain a true picture of the time and place.

Although nearly all such sketches were humorous in intent, for mining-town papers were expected to provide their readers with entertainment, as well as news, the pictures they conjure up have the ring of authenticity, as, for example, this one enumerating the sounds that were nightly to be heard in Pony Canyon:

This is a musical community. Through every night, far on into the small hours of the morning, may be heard the sweet squeak of the fiddle, the enchanting tones of a piano with a cold in its head, the dulcet strains of the accordion and concertina, the harmonious melody of the hand-organ, occasionally set off and elaborated by the martial strains given forth by a brass band. Singing is usually added to the charming collection of sounds, which, from the peculiar acoustic properties of the canyon in which Austin is situated, can be heard throughout the town; and in what should be the small hours of the night, voices can be heard trying to outscreech a Chinese bagpipe, to the tune of "Little Sweetheart, Come and Kiss Me," or "Who Will Care for Mother Now?" which tunes, by the way, don't harmonize very well with the bagpipe's notes.

All this is very pleasant for people who have murdered their families and can't sleep, and instead of soothing the savage breast, it sets the Indians in the camps on the surrounding hills to howling as if every mother's son of them was laboring under an attack of cramp colic. Then the cats and dogs add their voices to the melody, and unmusical people lie abed and listen, and wonder how many cases of murder and suicide will be reported next morning, and reflect how easy it would be for them to bring in a verdict of justifiable homicide if they happened to get on a jury to try a man for killing two or three of the musicians.

Or consider this paragraph dealing with an incident by no means uncommon in the lives of mining town editors:

"Throw your eye over that!" shrieked a voice behind us. And then a chunk of rock was slammed down on the table on which we were writing, just missing the funnybone of our arm. Our first thought was that it was one of those fellows come to inquire "who wrote that article?" and we were about to reach for our trusty mitrailleuse when the voice said: "How's that for richness?" and we knew that it was only a prospector come to display a specimen of a rich find. We picked up the piece of rock, scanned it carefully, and then asked our visitor where it had come from. "You can say it's an entirely new deestrick," he replied, "never afore trod by the foot of a white man. I call it Fortunate William. You see, I go by the name of Lucky Bill; but that's too common and vulgar-like to slap onto a mine." The specimen was composed principally of granite, with here and there a speck of quartz, and it looked as if it would assay about six-bits a ton. "What do you think she'll go?" asked our visitor. . . . We told him we were not a good judge of ore, and could not form an estimate of the value of the rock. "Well," said he, "I *am* a judge of ore; I've prospected every camp from Arizony to Montany, and I can jest tell you that that air rock won't go a cent under ten thousand dollars a ton." Then he told me the location of the district in which his ledge was situated, declaring that the vain was a "well-defined ledge," sixteen feet wide by actual measurement, free-milling ore, wood and water plentiful, and that he honestly believed it to be the second Comstock; and concluded by requesting us to "give her a hist in the paper," as he wanted to "attract the attention of capitalists." Then he unbuttoned his shirt, and, thrusting his hand within, rummaged around until he found a dilapidated cigar, which he handed to us, saying: "Thar, take that, and set her up as high as your language will go." We declined the cigar (because it was such a poor one, and smashed besides), saying that we did not expect remuneration for representing to the world the mineral resources of Nevada, and particularly of this section. "All right," he said, as he returned the cigar . . . "but I want you to understand that I ain't one of them ducks that wants editors to puff their mines for nothin'; thar ain't nothin' mean about me, and if you want the cigar you're welcome to it." We again declined the gift, and he left, after extracting from us a promise that we would "set her up high."

Something of the mining-town custom of bestowing descriptive names on one and all, and of the complications that occasionally resulted, is set forth in the following:

A respectable looking gentleman, just arrived from the Eastern States, was round town today, trying to find a man named Smith. There are several members of the Smith family in Austin, so the old gentleman experienced some difficulty in finding the exact Smith he wanted, and we are not positive that he has found him yet. Probably possessed of the somewhat prevalent idea that small boys know everything, he accosted one, and, addressing him as "my son," asked him if he knew anybody in this town by the name of Smith.

"Smith?" said the boy, "which Smith do you want? Le's see, — there's Big Smith and Little Smith, Three-fingered Smith, Bottle-nose Smith, Cockey Smith, Six-toed Smith, San Joaquin Smith, Lying Smith, Mushhead Smith, Jumping Smith, One-legged Smith, Fighting Smith, Red-headed Smith, Sugar-foot Smith, Bow-legged Smith, Squaw Smith, Drunken Smith, El Dorado Smith, Hungry Smith, and I don't know but maybe one or two more."

"My son," said the gentleman, "the Smith I am in search of possesses to his name none of the heathenish prefixes you have mentioned. His name is simply John Smith."

"All them fellows is named John," screeched the boy, as he drew his six-shooter and ran to the other side of the street to get a good shot at a passing Chinaman.

The old gentleman mused for a moment, then walked into a blacksmith shop and asked to see a city directory.

That all was grist to the editor's mill is abundantly clear from the following items, culled from among scores like them in the yellowing files of the *Reveille:*

We have heard a number of people complain that this has been a dull day; but we have failed to see it. A freight train arrived; several loads of wood passed up Main Street; seventeen dogs were all barking at once at a cow on Court Street; a woman stubbed her toe against a plank on Union Street; a man dropped a four-bit piece through a crack in the sidewalk on Cedar Street; a cow ate up a whole garden on Sixth Street; there was a whirlwind on Virginia Street. If the day was dull with all these stirring events, we would like to see what folks call a lively one. But some men would say times were dull if their grandmother was to fall three thousand feet down a mining shaft.

A four-year-old boy related to us the details of a desperate encounter which a party of boys and girls had with a lizard on the hillside this morning. It was so thrilling that, in order to keep the printers in copy until the telegraph news comes in, we give it to our readers:

"I seed the lizard first, and all the girls was afraid. I frowed a great big stick at him, and he wun up on a wock and laid down dead. Then a little girl hit him with a wock, and didn't hit him, and I went up and poked him with a stick, and he got alive again and wun away, and we all wun'd after him and he wun into a hole, and I fell down and skinned my nose, and one of the girls lost her shoe and her mother spanked her when she got home, and we're all going up this afternoon to kill that lizard."

An Upper Austin man refuses to allow his daughter to attend church anymore. A few Sundays ago the preacher said in his sermon, "Love thy neighbor"; and the daughter followed the injunction and fell in love with a young man who lives in the house adjoining her father's, who earns only sixty dollars a month and board as engineer of a wheel-barrow in a livery stable, and sits up until three o'clock in the morning playing pedro. The father says if the preachers can't preach any better doctrine than for the girls to love every scrub who happens to live in the next house, he would rather his daughters would grow up without the consolations of religion.

A predatory cow made a raid on a clothes-line last evening, and before she was detected succeeded in eating two frilled skirts, three lace-trimmed chimi-whatyoucallems, and several pairs of striped stockings. As the cow stumbled over an embankment, an angry woman could be seen at its top, waving a broom in the air, and with an expression on her countenance which said, in language as plain as words could express it:
"What wouldn't I give if I could cuss like a man!"

Business is dull with the doctors as well as with other people. A prominent physician sat for several hours on a rock today, intently watching a house on the other side of the street. When an acquaintance passed and asked: "What are you camped there for, Doc?" his only reply was: "The man who lives in that house got a present of a box of green cucumbers from a friend in California this morning," and he resumed his gaze at the door, with an evident determination to be on hand at the first indication of family suffering.

A woman went into a Main Street store this morning, and purchased a pick-handle. No question was asked her by the polite clerk, and he did not even intimate a desire to know if she was going prospecting. But she volunteered the information that she intended to make her husband and that carroty-headed old cat understand that she was not dead yet, even if she did have a consumptive cough, a weeping eye, false teeth, a big bunion, and symptoms of the hip-complaint. There is one man in this town who will hear the tocsin of war sound soon.

A few days ago, a stranger at one of our restaurants asked for a napkin at dinner. The landlord refused to give him one.

"But," said the guest, "that man at the other table has one."

"That man is a regular boarder, and just got back from San Francisco, and I have to pamper him for a day or so; but it won't be long before he will be wiping his mouth on the table-cloth, and cleaning his nails with a fork, like the other gentlemen. No, stranger, we don't allow any style here as a regular thing, but we can't help ourselves sometimes."

A prominent citizen remarked, in a Main Street saloon this morning, that the town is so distressingly quiet it must be an immense labor for the reporter of the *Reveille* to think up lies to put in the paper. While we repel with scorn the insinuation that we would give publication to a lie in the columns of the *Reveille,* we admit that facts on which to base local news are as scarce as preachers at a horse race.

The extraordinary weather of this morning is dangerous to our institutions. It threatens to introduce the umbrella into our midst. The last man who ventured on our streets with an umbrella was promptly shot, but his corpse was not mutilated, like that of his predecessor. Since the completion of the Central Pacific Railroad the manners and customs of an effete Eastern civilization have one by one encroached on our isolation, driving the old pioneers further and further back into the fastnesses of the mountains; and now that the showers of March threaten to foist the deadly umbrella on an unwilling people, men look into each other's faces and ask: "What *is* this consarned country coming to, anyway?"

Tramps abound in Austin at present. They are depredatory, larcenous, and burglarious; and it would be well for owners of portable property, such as hot stoves and steam hoisting works, to keep a lookout on their goods, wares, and merchandise. . . . When tramps come around residences, pretending hunger and asking charity, invite

them to an interview with the wood-pile. If they accept
the invitation, it shows that they are willing to work for a
living; and after they have sawed and split eight or ten
cords of wood into stove size, it would be well to offer
them something to eat. If he refuses to tackle the wood-
pile, then he is a tramp, in all his native cussedness. In
this case set the dog on him, or stand him up against the
fence and pour hot water down his back, or get a six-
shooter and make a true fissure lead ledge in his carcass.
. . . The best protection of all, however, is to keep your
doors locked.

Ever striving to be helpful, the editor often favored his
readers with bits of advice on the conduct of their daily
lives, including hints on how to achieve concord within
the domestic circle.

According to some medical authorities [he wrote in
one such homily] more quarrels arise between husband
and wife from their sleeping together than from any
other cause. It is said that the eliminative nervous force
of one person is absorbed by sleeping with a person of
absorbent nervous force, and that the absorber will sleep,
while the eliminator will be restless, nervous, and sleep-
less. The electrical qualifications of the cerebro-magnetic
concatenations, the one being positive and the other, a
negative pole, so disturb the nervo-vitality of the eliminative functions, that two persons possessing these attri-
butes in an opposite degree are uncongenial in magnetic
equilibrium; and thus quarrels in bed between husband
and wife are the inevitable result. We have frequently
observed this phenomenon in our own experience, and

the only remedy we can suggest is for husband and wife each to sleep with somebody else.

The price of fresh oysters in Austin is twelve and a half cents each. They were out walking, and she remarked that she had observed in the *Reveille* that there were some fresh oysters in town.

"Do you read the paper carefully, my dear?" he asked.

She said she read all the fashion news, and all the murders, and the recipes for making cup custard and "floating island," and the divorce cases; but she would like to know what all that had to do with oysters.

"Well, you see, my dear," said he, "there's been a terrible contagion broke out among the oysters, and the newspapers are advising people not to eat them; it appears that the bivalvular structure of the animal's diaphragm has become affected by a species of parasitical conglomeration, which, reacting on the vitality of the muscular forces of the alimentary canal, produces a paralysis of the oysters' nervous and digestive functions to such an extent as to render them unfit for human food."

She said he was the best husband in the world to be so careful of her health, and she would go home and tackle the cold pork and cabbage left from dinner, as she felt rather faint. He saw her home, and then went to the restaurant and had two dozen raw and a bottle of ale; and as he plunked the money on the counter, he remarked that fresh oysters were a necessary luxury, but it was like swallowing silver coin to eat them.

II

THE whims and foibles of Austin women were a frequent source of copy to the hard-pressed editor. Rarely did a day pass without an item or two on this favorite theme. Here are some samples:

A floating newspaper paragraph says that Mrs. Denison, the authoress, has made enough money out of "That Husband of Mine" to purchase a Washington residence. There is a woman in this town who has made enough money out of that husband of hers to purchase a set of furs on the installment plan. She did it while going through his pockets while he was asleep.

The story is told of an old lady who asked one of our physicians how a certain patient of his was getting along, and when the doctor informed her that the person in question was convalescent, she said:

"That's rough. Back yonder in the States, I knowed two wimmin and a crippled boy to die of convalescent. On one of the wimmin it broke out all over her in a rash, and it struck in and she died before you could bat your eye. But she made a beautiful corpse. They make nice corpses when they die of that, don't they, Doc?"

The doctor said he believed so.

She was a young lady from Reese River Valley, and her beau treated her to ice cream at one of the restaurants. She tried to eat the cream with knife and fork, and because she did not succeed, said it was "the most unsatisfyin' truck" she "ever seed," and asked the waiter if he wouldn't please warm it up a little.

"My husband is my idol," observed Mrs. Rubyrock to Mrs. Batterystamp. . . .

"Well," returned Mrs. B., "if he's any more idle than my old man I'd just like to see the shape of him. Why, my husband is that lazy that if he saw a twenty-dollar piece a-laying in the big road, he'd lay down alongside of it and go to sleep till I came along to pick it up for him."

A certain gentleman of this city had for a considerable length of time been keeping company with a young lady, and on the occasion of her birthday recently, sent her as a present a beautiful album. The lady was not at all satisfied with the gift, as she had expected something which would be significant of matrimonial intentions on the part of the gentleman — an engagement ring, or something in that line. She confided her dissatisfaction to her bosom friend, and said she thought her beau might have sent her "something binding." This remark the bosom friend communicated to the gentleman in the case, who was equal to the emergency, and immediately sent the dissatisfied lady a present of seven pounds of cheese.

An Upper Austin woman, who heard that a Cedar Ravine woman had been talking about her, told all her acquaintances that she intended to spit in that hussy's eye the first time she caught sight of her, and when they met she walked right up to her, put her mouth close up to the "hussy's" and — kissed her right on the lips, and said:

"Oh, my dear, I'm so glad to see you; and how are all the children, and has the baby got through teething yet?"

An old lady of this city, whose daughter reads a great many dime novels, hearing some persons conversing about the Centennial, said her Maria ought to know all about it, for she "just keeps the whole family busted buying them 'Ten-cent-ial' novels."

"What's the news up your way?" asked a down-town woman of an Upper Austin woman in a Main Street store today.

"Oh, not a thing in the world," replied the one questioned; "you see, we're awful quiet, peaceable people up our way, and of course I stay to home so much I don't know what's going on, anyhow, 'cause I have so much to do to 'tend to my children, and the sewing, and washing, and cooking; but they do say that Mrs. Bustem has got a brand-new silk dress, and nobody knows how she got it, and her husband only a common chlorider, and hasn't had a crushing in four months, and his last rock didn't pay for milling; and that Mrs. Gabble and Mrs. Tattle has had the worst kind of a fight, and when Mrs. Tattle made a grab at Mrs. Gabble's hair it was false, and all came out; and Mr. Squeezem chucked his wife out of doors 'cause she lammed the servant girl for letting him kiss her in the wood-shed; and that Mr. Sinchem drew a six-shooter on Mr. Bilkem for saying his wife said that his wife couldn't have no new bonnet this fall, 'cause her husband was poorer than Job's turkey, and couldn't pay ninety cents on the dollar if his creditors was to come down on him tomorrow and sell him out at a forced sale.

Oh, I tell you, we're awful peaceable people up our way; only it's tedious living in a neighborhood where there ain't nothing going on."

It was not alone during Hart's term as editor that Austin's ladies made frequent appearances in the columns of the *Reveille*. Thus, in the issue of January 17, 1865, appeared this philosophical comment:

THE BRUTE. — Eaves-dropping is naughty, but we can't help doing it, especially when a pretty woman talks. As one such passed our office last night, we heard her tell her companion that she had just had a terrible row with "George," and all because she wanted to kiss him and he wouldn't. We fear this brute George is the woman's husband. Unless the fair one has been partaking copiously of garlic, George deserves to be penned up with Marshal Bodrow's dogs, without benefit of habeas corpus.

By no means all the items, however, were in this vein; frequent reference was made to the activities of public-spirited members of the fair sex in making plans for civic betterment. When, in the spring of 1864, a group of Austin ladies, concerned over the lack of proper educational facilities in the new camp, launched a campaign to raise funds to build a permanent school building, the *Reveille* warmly supported this project. Having announced, on April 26, that "The Ladies of Austin" were to give a benefit supper the following evening at a local restaurant, to be followed by "dancing at Mrs. Graham's," the proceeds to go to the School Fund, the editor commented:

Citizens, particularly old bachelors, should remember the ball, and liberally purchase tickets for so praiseworthy a purpose. The movement is very generously and energetically conducted by the ladies, whose persuasive eloquence, in a cause that enlists their heartfelt sympathies, has transferred the price of numerous tickets from the coarse wallets of the gents to their pretty purses. It is certainly worth the price, even should one not attend the ball, to be visited by the fair ones, and so politely and smilingly persuaded to buy a ticket at the low price of two dollars. . . .

Evidently most of the town's solvent males responded nobly, for in its next number the paper announced that the net profit of the supper and dance amounted to "nearly $1000," and soon thereafter the building of the town's first school got under way.

There were, then and later, a considerable number of women in Austin who belonged to another social sphere than the ladies mentioned above. Although, as a family journal, the *Reveille* customarily maintained a discreet silence concerning the activities of these daughters of joy, occasionally something transpired in their parlors, a shooting or knifing or other forms of carnage, newsworthy enough to find its way into print. On May 2, 1864, however, one such lady achieved a fleeting notoriety for a different reason:

A woman of easy virtue went into a gambling house yesterday and, giving the barkeeper a check on Wells, Fargo & Co., for $400, asked for $100 on it, with which to "buck" the game. She fought the tiger and lost her hundred, when she asked for and obtained another hundred; this she likewise lost, also another hundred. Then she asked for the last hundred, with which she attacked the tiger at another table, at which she was successful. She won back all she had lost and something over. As she was leaving the house, it was discovered that the check was not endorsed, and a pen was secured for her to sign it, when she suddenly snatched the check and, putting it in her pocket, told the people of the house that they might all go to a very warm country, which she named. We have not heard that she was arrested.

Early Austin's wide-open gambling resorts were, like its brothels, seldom mentioned in the chaste columns of the *Reveille*, yet they were long a conspicuous feature of the life of the town. A. D. Richardson, a correspondent for the *New York Tribune*, who passed that way in the fall of 1865, thus described them:

At night the brilliantly lighted gambling saloons, with open fronts, are filled with a motley crowd. Women conduct the games at several monte tables, shuffling the cards and handling the piles of silver coins with the unruffled serenity of professional gamblers; while men of all classes "fight the tiger" with the usual earnestness of that fascinating pursuit.

The women of the Shoshone and Piute tribes who, with their love of bright garments, added a dash of color to Austin's drab streets, were also a dependable source of copy to the *Reveille's* roving reporter. On December 19, 1863, appeared this brief item:

The females among the Shoshones seem to be as inveterate gamblers as the males. Nearly every day parties of them can be seen squatted in the streets or on some hillside, playing cards for a few half-dollars piled up before them, seemingly enjoying the exciting game fully as much as their dusky lords.

During Fred Hart's term as editor he wrote numerous brief sketches of the local Indian maidens, of which the following are typical:

We did not attend the grand ball given by the Piutes to the Shoshones in Crow Canyon last night; but Captain Steve [chief of the local Shoshones] informs us that it was a grand success, and that Pine-nut Jane was the belle throughout the early part of the evening; but that, unfortunately, she became involved in a game of Indian poker with Horned-toad Sally, in which she lost her gorgeous attire on a queen-full, and her place as belle was taken by the aforesaid Sally. Steve says everything passed off peaceably. "No dlinkum whisakee; no fightum."

A squaw in a millinery store, purchasing a new "bunnit" to wear at the fandango, which shortly comes off at Stillwater, was what this reporter beheld last evening. She was as fastidious and as hard to please as a white woman is when engaged in a similar pastime, and tried on, and looked in the mirror to see how it became her, nearly every hat in the establishment. Having made her selection, she rolled it up in her handkerchief, and putting it under her arm, marched out of the store, saying to herself in the Indian tongue: "I'd just like to see the shape of the copper-colored woman that can put on more style than I can at the fandango."

A squaw sat down on the curb in front of the Post-Office this afternoon, and unrolling a bundle of calico, commenced to manufacture a dress. In less than an hour it was finished; and putting it on over her old clothes, she pulled out a pin here, a peg there, and untied a string in another place, made one step, and presto! the old clothes lay in the gutter. Gathering up the rags just shed, the daughter of the sagebrush cast one look of triumph at the spectators, and skipped gracefully off in the direction of the Indian camp, as proud as a Saratoga belle at the first ball of the season.

Some people think it very funny to chaff a squaw, but sometimes when the squaw talks back, they don't think it quite so funny. A case in point occurred in town the other day. A group of men were standing in front of a Main Street saloon, when a squaw leading a papoose came along. One of the party hailed the squaw with:
"Hello, Sally, whose baby is that?"
The daughter of the forest stopped and eyed her questioner, and then, pointing her finger at him, said earnestly:
"Him your papoose."
There was considerable laughter from the bystanders, but they were not laughing at the squaw.

Sam, the Indian who cleans the streets, has met with a severe bereavement in the loss of his oldest wife, who departed this life night before last. . . . Sam is grief-

stricken over the loss of his helpmate, and shed tears pro-
fusely while telling of it. Said he: "Him woman keep me
heap long time; me so sorry she die; other wife too
young; no got much sense; don't keep me as long as old
woman." Although he has got a young and pretty wife to
console him . . . Sam seems to feel very bad, and not to
entertain a very great affection for his living wife, who is
the best-looking Piute squaw in that portion of the tribe
resident here.

III

THE Indians, who had been roaming the arid hills and
sage-covered plateaus of central Nevada since long
before the coming of the white men, were still numerous
in the 1860's and later. Most of these were either
Shoshones or Piutes. The former, peaceable and indolent,
had for many generations occupied that area. They lived
in crude shelters called wickiups, made of poles set into
the ground and covered with ragged blankets or the skins
of animals, and — in their primeval state — subsisted on
rabbits, coyotes, snakes, and occasional fish caught in the
region's few streams, supplemented by nuts gathered in
the fall from the dwarf pine trees of the mountains,
which were roasted by the squaws and formed a staple
article of diet throughout the long winters.

The Piutes, on the other hand, were an energetic and
resourceful tribe who roamed over the broad region between the Rockies and the Sierra Nevada, and who on
occasion went on the warpath and launched bloody at-

tacks not only on the amiable Shoshones but on the white intruders. By the mid-1860's, however, ruthless counter measures by the settlers had in great measure stamped out the warlike proclivities of the Piutes and they, along with the Shoshones, had pitched their camps close to the settlements of the newcomers.

The town Indians [wrote Editor Hart in the late 1870's] subsist by begging at the kitchens of residences, hotels, restaurants, and miners' cabins, and the majority of them pass their time sleeping in the sunshine or gambling at cards. With all, gambling is the chief aim of life — whether it be Indian poker or monte, by day on the street corners, or at night in their miserable wickiups, or playing marbles "for keeps" among themselves, or with small white boys. Some of the men work at odd jobs, such as cutting firewood, scavenger work, washing dishes in restaurants or hotel kitchens, and other odd chores, while many of the women do rough washing for families and perform various easy menial services. The women are much more industrious than the men, but all their earnings go to their lords and masters, to furnish them with gambling capital.

The Indians were a picturesque feature of life in Austin all during the early years, and few reminiscences of the period fail to make mention of them. Thus, in the late 1860's, a young Kentuckian, Sam Osbourne, took his family up from San Francisco and installed them in a cabin on a shelf above the town. More than sixty years later, the daughter, Isobel Osbourne Field — whose mother, having divorced Osbourne, had meantime married Robert Louis Stevenson — recalled that groups of ragged Shoshones could frequently be seen peering through the cabin's uncurtained windows, offering an armful of firewood in exchange for a tin cup of coffee and a few pieces of bread.

Although, like most westerners of his generation, the Austin editor held no very high opinion of the aborigines, frequently referring to them as "lazy," "treacherous," and "nomadic loafers," he must nonetheless have been grateful for their presence in and about town, if only because they helped fill his daily columns of local news. The following items culled from many others on the subject, indicate how the white settlers of the day viewed the redskins.

A Piute passed down Main Street yesterday, whose appearance excited the attention of the white beholders, the jealousy of his male companions, and the admiring glances of the Indian maidens who were sitting on the curbstones pursuing investigations in natural history in their hair. He was mounted on a sleek pony, and was attired in a flaming red flannel shirt, two pairs of new blue overalls, a stiff-brimmed Peruvian sombrero, and a yellow linen duster, whose ample folds spread gracefully over the back of the pony, almost hiding it from view. As he rode along, he seemed to be aware that he was the admired of all admirers, and carried himself with an air of conscious pride, occasionally bestowing a contemptuous glance at some less fortunate Indian whose clothes were held together by bits of hay-rope, or vouchsafing a patronizing glance on the dusky maidens of his tribe.

. . . But Indian pride is as short-lived as that of his white brother; and it is sad to think that this noble red man, so happy yesterday, may have struck an Indian poker game last night, and today be a total wreck, with nothing to cover his manly form but an old plug hat and a lariat.

Human nature is the same the world over, and an Indian child takes as much pleasure in a doll as does a white one. We were amused this afternoon by observing a little Indian girl, apparently about three years old, who had found the head of a china doll . . . which she was fondling and nursing and talking to after the manner of all doll-mothers. Frequently we see in the streets little mites of Indian girls with miniature baskets, containing rag papooses, on their backs, which answer the same purpose to them as the most expensive and elaborately gotten-up doll does to a white child.

Yesterday an old Indian on Main Street was asked how old he was, and replied that he did not know.

"Do you savvy what year it is?" he was then asked.

"Yosh," he replied, "me heap savvy; *most* Injun he only savvy moon."

"Why Injun no count how old by moon?" asked the redman's questioner.

"Him too goddam lazy to count 'em," returned the brave.

"There," said a prominent citizen on Main Street this morning, pointing to an Indian who was carrying a sack of pine-nuts, "there you see the bounty of Nature to her children, the wise provision which she makes for these

untutored savages, who, living in a country to the eye
barren of all that is necessary to sustain life, yet find in
these sterile hills the means of subsistence in the nutri-
tious pine-nut. The pine-nut," he continued, "grows only
in countries possessing characteristics such as we find in
Nevada; and just look at it, how, by a generous Nature,
it is planted here and flourishes to ripeness for the benefit
of the aboriginal inhabitants."

"Ye-s," replied a bystander, "but if Nature wanted to
be so powerful particular about furnishing grub for these
Indians, what made her plant the red cusses in such a
God-forsaken country as this in the first place?"

The other said that the forces of Nature were so im-
mutable, and cause and effect were so hidden in the deep
recesses of mystery, that science had never been able to
penetrate them, and he guessed he couldn't answer that
question till he had consulted the authorities.

A resident of Austin has an Indian employed in chop-
ping wood at his residence, and that the aforesaid is an
aborigine who goes through the world with his eyes open
is evidenced by what follows.

Yesterday [Sunday] the Indian refused to chop any
wood, and when his employer asked him the reason . . .
he replied:

"Heap no work on Sunday; all same whitta man, heap
play poker."

The Indian children, less fortunate than the white ju-
veniles, are, except in a few isolated instances, unable to
procure the luxury of a sled. They take great delight in
coasting, but for them to even wish for a sled is to launch

out in the direction of the unattainable. To make up for this deprivation, they have invented a cheap and simple contrivance for coasting, which, though less comfortable and more dangerous than a sled, enables them to pursue the sport after a fashion. This coasting apparatus consists simply of a barrel stave, and a piece of rope or stout cord fastened through a hole in one end of the stave. They stand with the right foot on the stave, facing the string, which they hold in their hands, and by its means guide their craft; and giving themselves a start by pushing the left foot on the ground, go scooting down the steep track in the position taken by a boy skating on one skate. They get frequent falls and many bumps, but the little wretches are as tough as a pine-knot, and are heedless of the mishaps that befall them. Necessity is as much the mother of invention to the redskin as she is to his white brother.

Like their ancestors since time immemorial, Austin's Indians were congenital nomads who were rarely content to remain in one place more than a few weeks before gathering up their belongings and moving in a body to some new location, which might be another campsite only a few miles distant, or hunting or fishing grounds so remote that it took the caravan days or weeks to reach it. The scene at the local camp as the redskins prepared for one of these mass migrations was described by the *Reveille* in these words:

About six o'clock in the evening a great commotion was observable, bucks, squaws, and papooses all being at work pulling down the wickiups and packing the horses with the household goods. Viewed from the opposite hill, the preparations for departure presented a picturesque sight. The ponies standing patiently to receive their burden of high-colored blankets, provisions, cooking utensils, and the miscellaneous traps that go to make up an Indian household; papooses in all stages of raggedness tumbling about on the ground; squaws taking down the dirty and ragged odds and ends which serve for the covering of an Indian house; bucks riding furiously over the steep hillside to get the horses together — all set off against the grayish background of the hills with the sinking sun casting a glow on the scene that made bright color look brighter, and dirty bits of cloth look clean. It was a pretty picture at a distance; a near approach destroyed the romance and picturesqueness. . . . About eight o'clock the cavalcade began to move, the braves and favorite squaws and children, who were mounted, taking the trail around the hill above the Clifton grade, and the blear-eyed old squaws, with burdens on their backs, taking the shorter cut over the mountain; and by the time it was fairly dark there was not an Indian left in the town or its immediate vicinity.

Although throughout the 1870's and later, references to the Indians of the Austin area usually pictured them as shiftless, dirty, but otherwise inoffensive members of the community, this had not always been so. During the early days of the camp, before the redskins had adopted the ways of civilization, they were regarded with suspicion by the white settlers, and from time to time as sources of imminent danger.

Thus, in 1865, a situation arose that caused grave concern throughout central Nevada and, in particular, to those living on isolated ranches or in remote mining camps. For word had reached the authorities that a band of Piutes were plotting a series of raids on such settlers, and had sent agents among the normally peaceable Shoshones to persuade them to join in a foray designed to drive the intruders from their traditional hunting grounds. The situation was considered a serious one, for the army posts in the territory had been stripped of their garrisons, the troops having been recalled to the east coast on the outbreak of the Civil War.

Hearing that a large number of Shoshones had gathered at a point in the Reese River Valley while they debated the question of whether or not to join the Piutes, Nevada's first governor, H. G. Blaisdel, hurried to Austin from the state capital at Carson City. Then, having been joined by a group of leading citizens of the town, the delegation proceeded up the valley to the Shoshones' camp. Although the party was greatly outnumbered, Blaisdel and his companions made their way to the center of the conclave. There the Governor addressed the assemblage, pointing out the many indignities the tribe had suffered at the hands of the Piutes, who had driven the Shoshones out of their ancestral hunting grounds, kidnaped their most comely squaws, and committed numerous other outrages.

At first, the Shoshones listened to the harangue in stony silence; however, when Blaisdel went on to state that representations were being made to the Great White Father in Washington urging greater assistance to the peace-loving tribe, and assuring them that the state militia would protect them from further raids by the Piutes, grunts of approval began to be heard. Eventually, the Governor's eloquence won the day. The pipe of peace was brought forth and smoked by Blaisdel and the ranking Shoshone chiefs, and the threat of Indian warfare was averted.

That the Austin Indians were not lacking in the guile traditionally ascribed to their race is indicated by a dramatic episode that took place early in the present century. In the fall of 1899, residents of the Reese River country were shocked to learn that a particularly brutal crime had been committed in the area. Someone had appeared at the house of a track repairman on the railroad between Austin and Battle Mountain and, while the husband was absent at work, beat to death the wife and their year-old daughter, using a jagged piece of rock as the lethal weapon.

The murderer did not remain long at large, for he, a young Indian named Frank, confessed the crime to his father, and the latter turned his son over to the sheriff's posse. The prisoner was taken to Austin where, after a brief trial, he was convicted and sentenced to death by hanging. While he was lodged in the Lander County jail awaiting the carrying out of the court's order, a group of local Indians one night raised a mighty disturbance, staggering about the streets and filling the air with their drunken shouts until they were rounded up by the sheriff and confined overnight in the one-cell jail.

Soon after the disturbers were released the following morning, the condemned man was heard to be moaning in his cell and, although a physician was summoned, he died soon afterwards. An autopsy was ordered, which revealed that the dead man's stomach contained a quantity of a substance that was identified as wild parsnip, a highly poisonous plant which grows beside the streams of central Nevada, the lethal qualities of which were well known to the Indians of the area. It thereupon grew clear to the officials that the wily redskins had pretended drunkenness in order to gain access to the jail and so provide their countryman with means of circumventing the white man's justice.

IV

A NUMEROUS group of Chinese found their way into the town during its early days, where, as in other places all over the west, they established their own quarters, lived much to themselves, and found employment operating laundries and stores, cooking in restaurants, peddling vegetables from door to door, and similar tasks.

The editors of the *Reveille*, although, like most westerners of the period, they held no high opinion of the Orientals, nonetheless found them fully as fruitful a source of copy as the Indians, as indicated in the items that follow. The first, a sketch of one native of the Flowery Kingdom well known in the town, bore the title "Hans."

There is a barber shop in Austin conducted by Germans, and in their employment is a Chinaman whom they have dubbed "Hans." He is an observing Celestial, and, like all of his race, apt in learning American customs and phrases. The Chinese are notoriously imitative, and about the first thing American they learn is how to swear. Their native vocabulary has no words of such strong emphasis as the Nevada oath, and consequently the acquisition of a language containing words that enable a man to give full expression to his true feelings is one of the greatest boons the Mongolian has gained by his contact with our superior civilization. Hans is doubly fortunate in this respect; for, in addition to his knowledge of nearly all the leading American expletives, he has a fair store of the most elaborate German oaths, and can swear grammatically in the two languages with dialectic variations.

He is quite a philosopher in his way, and loud in denunciations of the leading vices and sins of his race. Among other things, he abhors opium-smoking. . . . Knowing the strong opinions entertained by Hans on this subject, and having myself seen its effects in the lack-luster eyes and wretched faces of those whites who are addicted to the habit, I one day questioned him as to the effects of the use of the drug on his countrymen. His reply was prompt, terse, and to the point. Said he:

"Chinaman smoke opium one year, he all same monkey, all same white man"; a comparison I did not appreciate, but which served to show that a frank answer is not always flattering.

Hans is also opposed to the female slavery practices of his countrymen. The Chinese who immigrate to America are seldom accompanied by their families. They do not come here to remain, and therefore have no home ties. The majority of the males are brought to this country under a system of coolieism, which, although not actual slavery, is the next thing to it. But the women who come are absolute slaves, having a high value as chattels, varying with age, physical attractions, and condition. They are imported by the wealthy Chinamen of San Francisco — if not directly by the "Six Companies," which control all the Chinese in America — and the purpose of their importation is the vilest that can be conceived.

Hans is about the only Chinaman whom I ever heard denounce this infamous system. He says it is "too muchee bad; sell woman all same Melican man sell mule"; and he expresses a determination never to own one of his countrywomen by this method. Talking about matrimony, he said:

"Me get lich, me go Chiny, make love tiptop Chiny girl; heap marry him, all same white man."

But when asked if he would bring his wife to this country, he replied:

"Not by damn sight. Some dam tiefee Chinaman stealee him and sell him."

Once, a Chinaman passing the shop where Hans is employed, and seeing him engaged in putting a shine on a customer's boots, derisively called him something that sounded like "Tu-na-ma-hing — highlowjackandthegame," which Hans afterwards explained was Chinese for bootblack. Hans immediately replied in good, solid English, "Go to blazes, you rat-eating scrub!" and in a tone that indicated the utmost contempt for everything wearing pig-tails, "Me no wash-woman Chinaman."

The Chinese of the town, like those elsewhere, were inveterate gamblers, and the *Reveille* frequently called attention to this weakness, and to the fact that other residents, both whites and Indians, often sat in at their games.

Owing to the high license fees levied on banking games by the state laws [stated an item in the mid-1870's] the Chinese of Austin no longer play their national game of "Fan-Tan," but have substituted therefor the good, old-fashioned North American draw-poker. Every night, when the hour arrives for business, a Celestial stands on the single street of Chinatown, and, in a voice that can be heard throughout the quarter and the neighborhood surrounding, proclaims that the game is open to all comers. The proclamation is uttered in Chinese, and freely translated is as follows:

"Hear ye! Hear ye! The poker game in the Chinese quarter, in and for Lander County, State of Nevada, is now open; free for all, without regard to age, sex, or previous condition of servitude. Come one, come all — white, black, yellow, and copper-colored — and take a hand in the game of the barbarian."

When the crier has concluded, the Chinamen rush into the house where the game is played, and the business commences. There is scarcely a night that white men may not be seen, side by side with Chinese, deep in the mysteries of poker; and, though the white players cannot translate the words of the proclamation, they know by the sound and by instinctive feeling that it is a solemn announcement of the opening of the game.

Even the Indians have grievances against the Chinese [states another paragraph]. Captain Thompson, the Piute oracle, came into the *Reveille* office this morning, and inquired if it was the intention of the whites to drive the Chinamen out of town. It was explained to him that the white people desired to get rid of the Celestials, but by peaceable means. This did not seem to suit Thompson, and he indignantly exclaimed:

"No good! Why no white man heap kill dam Chinaman? Chinaman heap all same bad."

When asked in what particular the Asiatics were so bad, he said:

"Him Chinaman too damn schmart (smart) — all time heap cheat 'em Injin play poker."

The *Reveille* sanctum was honored this forenoon by a visit from the chief justice of the Piute tribe . . . Judge John, as he calls himself. The judge is the most intelligent Indian we have ever met . . . and seems to be pretty well posted on matters and things. . . . He asked us our views on the coming Presidential election [the Hayes-Tilden contest of 1876] and wound up by giving us his opinion on the Chinese Question. Said he:

"Chinaman no good — he come here, heap work, no spend'em money; but tak'em all money 'way over big water. Injin . . . no like 'em Chinaman; heap down on 'em. Too many Chinaman come San Francisco, Virginny [Virginia City] — all United States; heap work for little money; whita man, whita woman, and Injin no got work. Bimebye heap kill'em Chinaman; send 'em back home."

The ancient beliefs and customs of the Orientals, so bizarre and heathenish to the eyes of the Austin whites, also came under the all-seeing eye of the town's newspaper. Thus:

The Chinese are firm believers in necromancy, fortunetelling, and kindred arts. Several Chinamen in this city make a profession of fortune-telling. Their method is to take a smoke of opium, from the effects of which they have visions, from which they interpret whether certain sick persons will die or get well, or whether certain individuals will win or lose at gambling games. . . . They have a small ivory figure to assist them. . . . If the seer's prognostications are verified, he is a smart fellow; if not, the blame is laid on the god.

Yesterday being the last of the Chinese New Year, the heathen gave a grand jubilistic blow-out, and made the night hideous with the notes of the one-stringed fiddle, the gong, the tom-tom, the Chinese bagpipes, and other ear-splitting instruments of their native land. At midnight the entire population united in singing the Chinese national hymn, which sounded like the expiring howls of three thousand poisoned dogs, with variations by several hundred feline musicians. The music and the firing of bombs and crackers was kept up almost until daylight; and many a man who before was indifferent to the Chinese question, arose this morning from his restless couch and expressed a determination to sign a petition for the immediate abrogation of the Burlingame treaty.

The 21st instant is the Chinese festival of something or other, when they decorate the graves of their dead with roast pigs, cups of tea, rice, confections, and other Chinese delicacies. As in this country a license tax is affixed to almost everything, John got it into his collective head that he would be required to take out a license to feed his dead, and a delegation waited upon the City Marshal to inquire "how muchee licee?" The officer gave them permission to hold their festival without money and without price, and on the date mentioned the graves will be decorated in accordance with Chinese custom. This will offer to the numerous tramps now in Austin a most magnificent opportunity for a moonlight picnic — if the coyotes don't get there ahead of them.

Humorous squibs about John Chinaman often helped fill the columns of "Local Jottings" on dull days, as for example:

Out at the Chase Mine, New York Canyon, the miners have been greatly troubled by mountain rats. They have been a particular source of annoyance to the Chinese cook, and he had vowed by all the gods of the Flowery Kingdom to wreak a bitter vengeance on the first marauding rodent which should fall into his clutches. Last Saturday, while busily engaged in cutting meat for the morning's hash, he heard a rustling noise, and looking around, saw what he supposed to be a rat's head protruding through a crack in the floor. Seizing a carving fork, and gliding stealthily up to the object, he plunged it into its body, and, with a yell of triumph, uplifted the impaled animal exclaiming, "Me catchee dam rat!" The miners, hearing his cries, rushed into the kitchen; but paused on the threshold, for they smelt a smell. About this time, the Chinaman smelt something too, and exclaiming, "Hi yah, me smellee hell!" dropped the fork, and broke from the room. The animal he had impaled was one of the genus known scientifically as *Mephitis Americana,* vulgarly termed a skunk.

A few nights ago, a Chinaman was coming up on the stage from Battle Mountain. He was thinly clad, having no warmer clothes than a regulation Chinese blouse and trousers, and being destitute of blankets. The night was fearfully cold, and the Celestial suffered severely; but for a long time he bore the hardship with the meekness and patience so characteristic of his race. He tried to sleep, and snuggled down on the floor with his head under one seat and his feet under the other; but the pitching and rolling of the stage over the cut-up and frozen roads bumped him unmercifully, until at last even his Chinese stolidity gave way, and he rose from his uncomfortable position on the floor, and seating himself on the front seat, said to the other passengers:

"Hell dam! Thissee lodgee house no good!"

A delegation of Chinese waited on the City Marshal today, and preferred a request that he lock up members of the Sazerac Lying Club in the City Jail until after the souls of the dead Chinamen had had a chance at the food they intended to pile on the graves of those departed Celestials today. The Marshal could find nothing in the city charter and ordinances authorizing such a proceeding, and the Chinamen concluded to stuff the pigs and chickens with nitro-glycerine and garlic.

Two Chinamen entered the telegraph office this morning, and inquired the cost of a telegram to Hongkong . . . as they said that some cousins of theirs were passengers on the ill-fated steamer *Japan*. The operator informed them that the cost would be in the neighborhood of $100, when one of them exclaimed:

"Me no send 'em; hundled dollah too muchee for dead Chinaman!"

A Chinese merchant came into the *Reveille* office this morning to purchase some paper, and while waiting . . . asked us if we had heard of the "big Chinaman fight in Virginny." On our replying in the affirmative, he heaved a deep sigh, and said:

"Him Chinaman allee same dam fool; him got littlee money; then him fight, and give allee him money to damn lawyer for makee talk; then him lawyer he too muchee talk, and Chinaman him bloke, and go washee for money for give him big mouf lawyer."

This particular heathen doesn't seem to entertain a very high opinion of the legal fraternity.

All Chinatown was drunk last night, owing to the copious potations of rice brandy indulged in by the Chinamen at a dinner in honor of the opening of the new store of the Fat Chung Company. During the night the Chinamen got up a game something on the principle of "Simon says thumbs up," and penalty being that the loser must take a drink of China brandy. White men were allowed to take part in the game, and one of them, as soon as he dropped on it that the loser had to take a drink, commenced throwing off and got stuck every time. His dodge was soon detected by the hosts, and before the white player had lost enough games to get up a respectable drunk, he was indignantly "barred out" of the game, and ignominiously "fired out" of the house.

Hong Sing claimed that Sam Hing owed him two hundred dollars; Sam Hing said he didn't, and both Celestials agreed to leave the matter to the arbitration of the heads of the different wash-house companies in town, who consulted together and pronounced a verdict that Hing must go down to the graveyard and cut off a rooster's head that he was not indebted to Sing . . . decreeing likewise that Hing should pay Sing $2.50 for taking the oath — a sort of notary's fee, as it were. In accordance with this verdict the parties litigant, in company with a number of other Chinamen, armed with knives, bludgeons, and six-shooters, repaired to the graveyard, where Hing decapitated the fowl and solemnly asserted that he didn't owe Sing a dog-gone cent. Sing paid Hing the $2.50 for taking the oath, and then foolishness was about to commence; but the City Marshal, who was on the watch, stepped in and read the riot act, and disarmed the party. . . . Had it not been for the interference of the Marshal there would have been bloodshed, and Hong Sing's bones would have been put in condition for shipment to the Flowery Kingdom. He remarked to the Marshal that "maybe so you no come, me no more washee."

CHAPTER FOUR

Grocer Gridley and His Sack of Flour

I

AUSTIN'S first municipal election was on April 19, 1864, and great were the preparations for the event. For in the eyes of the citizens, the adoption of a city charter and the choosing of officials to carry out its provisions would mark the transition of their little community from helter-skelter mining camp to orderly, up-and-coming American town.

But it was not this alone that stirred interest in the election to fever pitch. For by the spring of 1864 the long-drawn-out Civil War was nearing its climax, and in Austin, as elsewhere in the Territory, both the North and the South had their ardent partisans. Accordingly, each faction put up candidates for mayor and other municipal officials and waged spirited campaigns to put them into office. The *Reveille*, in its account of the party primaries at which the candidates were selected, commented that both mayoralty aspirants were estimable citizens, and pridefully pointed out that more than fifteen hundred ballots had been cast at the primaries, terming it "a pretty good vote for a one-year-old town."

Because, as we shall see, Austin's first election had con-

sequences of far more than local importance, much was
written about the campaign, both by contemporary scribes
and those of later date. One version, that of J. Ross
Browne, who visited the scene a little more than a year
later, thus pictured the situation:

Republicans and Copperheads were pretty evenly di-
vided; and the state of feeling between them was exceedingly lively, if not hostile. A great deal of betting took
place on the test questions, the chief of which was the
election of Mayor. Every man felt not only a local and
personal but a national interest in the result. The two candidates were well matched. On the Democratic side was
David E. Buel — "Unce Dave," as his fellow-citizens fa-
miliarly called him — a man of imposing presence, six feet
four, and large in proportion, without a fault save that of
being always on the wrong side, and with a frank, generous, off-hand way about him that was wonderfully attractive to the honest miners. A more popular candidate
could not have been chosen to give strength to a bad
cause. . . . The other candidate was Charles Holbrook,
a young man of excellent character and fine business
capacity. Holbrook had just erected a handsome store,
built of cut granite, and was one of the leading merchants.
His integrity was undoubted, his intelligence of a superior
order, and his political faith ultra-Union. Betting was the
order of the day. Each party was confident of success.

In its issue for April 19, the morning of the election, the
Reveille devoted half a column to happenings of the evening before, during which both candidates and their sup-
porters had marched up the slanting main street in blocks-

long torchlight processions behind the town's brass band. "It is seldom," the editor commented, "that so great an interest is manifested in a city election; however, it is entirely political, the division being strictly upon national politics, the candidates upon either side being very popular, irrespective of party. The demonstrations," he added, "must have been very expensive to some one . . . but it was great fun for the crowd."

Ever on the alert to counteract efforts of rival mining town editors to minimize Austin's importance, the *Reveille* did not fail to draw a moral from the large sums local citizens had wagered on the outcome. Two days later — the Union candidate, Charles Holbrook, having won by a narrow margin — appeared this item:

It is commonly asserted, particularly in the correspondence of California papers, that there is no money in Austin. The great display of gold, offered and staked upon the success of the rival candidates, gives the lie to assertions of our poverty. Many thousands of dollars changed hands on the result. One man is reported to have lost upwards of $5000, and there are but few Democrats who are not poorer now by numerous double-eagles. Following our suggestion in reference to the Sanitary Fund, a box was prepared and about $60 donated. This is a very insignificant sum, but it seemed as if everyone saved his money for the purpose of betting. . . .

The Sanitary Fund to which this somewhat testy reference was made, was a forerunner of the Red Cross, a country-wide movement to raise funds to buy food, clothing, and medical supplies for sick or wounded soldiers in army hospitals and rest camps. The *Reveille* from the beginning had vigorously supported this campaign. In late March, it had urged that Austin participate by donating silver bricks, the products of its booming mines, and forwarding them to a national fair to be held for the benefit of the fund at St. Louis in May. On April 7, a second reminder had appeared in its columns:

We hear nothing in response to the call made for subscriptions to the St. Louis Fair for the benefit of the Sanitary Fund. There is yet time, and will not some public-spirited citizens take the lead and start the ball rolling? Our citizens have as yet done but little toward assisting in so benevolent a project. . . . At the same time we will be presenting to the world evidences of our wealth and resources that will return, in benefits to the country, a thousand percent upon the amount we would bestow.

Evidently this second attempt to awaken local citizens to their responsibilities was no more successful than the first, for a week later the editor again brought up the subject. This time he based his appeal not only on the excellence of the cause but on the fact that by failing to support the campaign then in progress throughout Nevada, the Austinites were putting their town in a highly unfavorable light elsewhere in the Territory. Thus, an editorial in the issue for April 14 began:

From the Territory of Nevada has been sent to the Sanitary Fund about $50,000; of this sum Storey County [where Virginia City and the other Comstock towns were located] claims to have sent about $45,000. The County

Grocer Gridley and His Sack of Flour   125

of Lander has not yet placed its name on the list of con-
tributors, and is stigmatized by the Virginia papers as one
of the counties "of big pretensions and little liberality."

It is the duty of the people to contribute something to
the relief of the unfortunate soldier, and that duty rests
upon all, of whatever political party or section, who can
lay any claim to the possession of a feeling heart or a
liberal hand. The Sanitary Commission [of Nevada] will
not send the donations entrusted to its care until the 28th
inst., thus giving us ample time to render our tribute. . . .

The editor then went on to make a suggestion that was
to have consequences far greater than he could have fore-
seen:

We are soon to have a charter election [the editorial
concluded], the maiden election of our new city. How
better, or more auspiciously could we inaugurate our new
government than by making it a special point to do something for the benefit of the Sanitary Fund as we vote?
. . . We would suggest that some public-spirited individuals constitute themselves a committee and attend at
each ward polls to receive subscriptions, contributions
or orders for the same from voters. . . .

This suggestion was duly carried out, but as we have
seen with not very satisfactory results, a mere sixty dollars
having been deposited in the collection boxes at the poll-
ing places. However, Austin's support of the Fund was
not to be limited to that insignificant sum. On the day
following the voting yet another of the numerous election
bets was paid, and in a manner that was presently to make

front-page news all over the country. Two days after the election, on April 21, the *Reveille* told the story in detail:

Yesterday was a gala day in Austin, and one that will be remembered with pride and pleasure by all its citizens.

Two of our prominent men, Mr. R. C. Gridley, of the firm of Gridley, Hobart & Jacobs, as gallant a Copperhead as ever lived, and Dr. Herrick, one of our county officials, made a very amusing wager, the terms of which were, that should D. E. Buel, Democrat, be elected Mayor, Dr. Herrick would carry a fifty pound sack of flour through the Main Street, from the First Ward, Clifton, to the Fourth Ward, upper Austin, a distance of a little over a mile and a quarter, marching to the tune of "Dixie." The reverse was: "Should Charles Holbrook, Union, be elected, Mr. Gridley would carry the sack of flour from his store, in upper Austin, down the Main street to the First Ward, marching to the tune of "Old John Brown."

Yesterday morning the wager was paid in the most splendid style. At 10 o'clock a large convocation of citizens, with the Austin band, people on horseback, many flags of all sizes, were assembled about the store of Mr. Gridley, who was ready with his sack of flour trimmed with ribbons and mounted with a number of small flags. A procession was formed, with the city officers-elect, mounted on horseback, at the head, followed by Dr. Herrick carrying the coat and cane of Mr. Gridley, who was immediately behind, with the sack on his shoulder, with his son, a youngster of about ten years, carrying a small flag, marching beside him, and escorted by the Democratic Central Committee, two carrying flags, one a pole to which was attached a huge sponge, and the other holding high in the air a new broom; then came the band, playing "Dixie," leading an immense procession of citizens.

All marched down the street amid the most enthusiastic cheering of spectators and the screeching of whistles on numerous mills on the route. Upon reaching Clifton the principals, with the band and as many as could, marched into the Bank Exchange saloon, where the ceremony of delivering the flour, surrendering the flag and throwing up the sponge was performed, with most appropriate and graceful speeches by Messrs. Gridley, Marley, Worthington, and Herrick. It is not necessary to say that the spirits of the bar added some, if possible, to the enthusiastic spirit of the attending crowd. Cheers and tigers greeted the speakers, the throwing up of the sponge, the surrender of the flags and the broom. "A new broom sweeps clean," and the one transferred was new and large. It was typical of the clean sweep the party had made, and also that the course of the new officers of the new city would be like a new broom, and that in their term in office they would leave a clean record.

Nothing could exceed the good feeling with which the Democratic party surrendered its emblems, and the amiability with which they greeted their municipal rulers. When the ceremonies were completed, the procession again formed, now with the stalwart flour-carrier mounted on a fine horse, and with flags streaming and the band playing National airs, marched back to the front of Grimes & Gibson's saloon, where the generous proprietors invited all to enter and partake freely in honor of the occasion.

A stand was erected upon which the newly distinguished sack of flour was placed. After a few prelim-

inary remarks, Mr. Gridley offered for it two hundred
dollars, the money to be given to the Sanitary Fund. Mr.
T. B. Wade took the stand as auctioneer and the price of
flour went up to such heights as it had never before
reached even in starving times, or that the most successful speculator ever dreamed of getting. Double-eagles in
solid gold was the only currency that could buy flour at
the auction stand. From two hundred the price soon ran
up to three hundred and fifty and was declared sold. It
was said a Union man had bid that amount, but as he was
not very prompt in coming forward, Mr. Gridley offered
the money and desired the much-coveted flour. Mr. M. J.
Noyes, as a prominent Union man and a successful candidate for Alderman, claimed the right to pay the money
and handed out a bagful of twenties. Amid the deafening
cheers of the assemblage, the flour was delivered to him,
and immediately returned for sale, the proceeds to go, as
before, to the noblest of purposes, the Soldiers' Sanitary
Fund.

The auction still went on, with the precious flour sold
again and again until it had been sold for many times its
weight in silver. Mr. Buel, although defeated as a candidate, and a heavy loser of wagers, was determined not
to be outdone, but as his gold had run short, offered a
certificate of indebtedness of the United States Indian
Department, which would be paid in greenbacks, calling
for $1,115. This was the most liberal of all bids, but as
gold was the only article recognized as money, it was not
accepted. All bidders were cheered and the band saluted
them with patriotic tunes. When the prices fell as low as
twenty dollars, Mr. Gridley, for Gridley, Hobart & Jacobs,
again bid two hundred and was a purchaser.

Greedy and anxious now became the seekers of the valuable flour; the auctioneer became eloquent in its praise, and although the sufferings of the soldiers' life were most feelingly depicted, the cheers and unbounded hilarity of the audience evinced that there was no feeling of sadness among the listeners. When the twenties in the pockets of individuals ran short, combinations were made; the Democrats must buy, the Republicans must buy, the Odd Fellows bought, then the Masons must excel; there was no thought of party, or of rival societies, or of individual enmities, but only to excel in their contributions to the Fund.

Thus the sale went on with the many combinations to raise large amounts — the merchants attempting to surpass the hotel keepers, the mills, and saloons, mining companies, town proprietors, each determined not to be out-done; what with money, script, stocks, town lots, it appeared as if the whole property of Austin was about to be swallowed up in the maelstrom of the Fund. At a late hour in the evening, having continued since 12 o'clock noon, the sale was adjourned until today, when it will again be started at one hundred dollars, there being several starting bids at that sum.

At the time of the adjournment the amount of cash bids in the aggregate was $4,021, with accepted bids from D. E. Buel for one block of lots in the town of Watertown, and a large number of lots bid by Jeff Work. The amount of gold paid in as bids were made was $3,180. Stocks, certificates of indebtedness, and much other valuable property worth many thousands of dollars were also offered, but as they were not readily convertible into cash, were not accepted.

As the sale is to be continued today, we cannot publish a list of names until it is closed, but we will publish them in our next. In the meantime we would suggest that a careful revision of the list be made, so that none may be reported wrong, recollecting that, as Byron says, "Glory consists in being killed in battle and having your name reported wrong in the *Gazette.*"

A nobler objective never excited a more generous response, and we doubt if ever a sack of flour was so freely purchased at such great prices as the now celebrated GRIDLEY–HERRICK sack of the Reese River.

True to his promise, the editor, two days later printed the names of more than a hundred "persons, firms, and associations" that had bid on the by then famous sack of flour. The amounts ranged from four hundred dollars down to a minimum of ten dollars, with the majority — including the proprietors of the *Reveille* — contributing twenty dollars each. Before listing the donors, however, the story led off with this paragraph:

The gala day of Austin, following the Municipal Election, will long be remembered by the citizens. The great generosity and good feeling displayed was a happy inauguration of our city government. It is to be hoped that, commencing under such auspices, its future may be as prosperous as its beginning was pleasant. One day not being sufficient to sell the flour to all who wished to purchase, a portion of the following day was used in the sale. The amount of cash sales was $4,349.75, plus property of many thousands of dollars in value. The donations were placed in charge of a committee, which will assess the property and as soon as possible remit the amount received for it to the East. The property donated was as follows: D. E. Buel, one block in Watertown, consisting of eight lots; J. J. Work, two blocks in Rogers' addition to the city of Austin, consisting of sixteen lots; D. E. Buel, for the proprietors of the eastern addition of upper Austin, one block, consisting of eight lots; Keause & Fernbach, twenty-four quires of calf-bound blank books; and Adolph Falk, $24 in county script.

The *Reveille's* editor, recognizing that the auction deserved a lasting place in the annals of Austin, feared that its significance might presently be forgotten unless proper steps were taken. Having given the matter thought, he two days later offered this suggestion:

A PROPOSITION. — The first city election of Austin, the central and most promising town in Nevada, has transpired. The celebration of it has been characterized by a spirit of enthusiasm, hilariousness, generosity, and unique display, seldom equalled in any city. The carrying of a sack of flour through the streets, and its unexampled sale for a noble purpose, need a more lasting memorial than a passing newspaper record.

We would briefly propose that a competent draughtsman be engaged to prepare a certificate of sale of the famous sack, representing the great procession, manly carrier, &c. This is to be lithographed in a manner fit for framing, and filled out to purchasers of the flour, or sold to others who desire to keep a memento of the occasion. . . .

Nor did this proposal go unheeded. Although the method of commemorating Gridley's feat did not take precisely the form the paper had suggested, the honor was nontheless a high one, as this paragraph, published on June 12, makes clear:

CITY SEAL. — The great seal of the town of Austin is now in use by the Common Council. It is from a design made by Mr. Morris Locke, appropriate, simple, and inimitable. The coat of arms is simply a sack of flour bearing the motto: "Sanitary Fund $5,000," around which is a wreath surrounded by the words: "Common Council, City of Austin — Incorporated February 20, 1864." This makes a very pretty seal, and will perpetuate the memory of a singular and pleasant scene that attended the inauguration of the city of Austin.

Incidentally, this seal, which remained in active official use for more than a decade, dropped from sight after the town was disincorporated in the mid-1870's. After the seal had been forgotten for some eighty years, Jock Taylor, the *Reveille's* present editor, published an editorial in the summer of 1953, urging that an effort be made to locate the historic die. However, a diligent search has so far failed to bring it to light.

The paper's original suggestion, in April 1864, that Gridley's feat be commemorated by issuing a printed memorial did not fall on fallow ground. On June 15 appeared an item in its columns stating that: "An enterprising artist in San Francisco has taken friend Gridley's photographic phiz and the sack of flour in many different positions, and is now selling them for the benefit of the Sanitary Commission." Four days later it added that a supply of the photographs had been placed on sale in Austin and that they were "going like hotcakes."

II

BY THEN the Austin grocer and his much-auctioned sack of flour were widely known all over the west coast. For the Overland Telegraph had promptly spread abroad news of the Austin auction, and during the days that followed, many coast papers had carried editorials commenting on the novelty of the exploit and the substantial sum it had raised for the Fund. Some Nevada editors, however, particularly those of the Comstock area, where the rapid rise of the Reese River town was causing growing concern, greeted first reports of the exploit with marked skepticism. Thus, the *Daily News* at Gold Hill in reprinting the dispatch from Austin on April 22, prefaced its account of the auction with the remark that the news was "important if true."

A week later, however, on April 29, the Gold Hill paper, having grown convinced that the earlier reports were authentic, published this grudging tribute to the citizens of the rival town:

It is gratifying to perceive that the noble example set by the people of Storey county [where Gold Hill was located] in behalf of our suffering soldiery, is exciting the emulation of other counties in the Territory. The recent rather comical flour-selling operation out in Austin resulted in a splendid contribution to the patriotic fund, and most gloriously wiped out the stigma which had been too hastily cast upon the Reese River people. . . .

Comment in some west coast journals had a distinctly political slant, for dispatches from Austin had, of course, stated that the loser of the election bet had been a supporter of mayoralty candidate Buel, an avowed sympathizer of the South in the current conflict. Thus, the *Sacramento Star,* an ardently pro-Northern organ, published this caustic paragraph toward the end of May:

QUERY. — 'Tis said that Gridley, the Austin Sanitary sack-of-flour man, is a Copperhead, and bet on the election of Buel, the Secesh candidate. If such is the case, is this snug little sum of thirty-six thousand dollars [the total amount thus far raised in the Territory] safe in his hands? As far as we are concerned, we prefer not to trust either Copperheads or traitors with even hot stoves, much less with the people's thousands contributed to aid the sick and wounded of our armies. What assurance have we that the money will not be misapplied?

In its issue for May 29, the *Reveille,* having quoted the above, offered this vigorous rejoinder:

The remarks of the *Star* seem very improper under the circumstances, and we believe that on sober second thought it will make whatever amends are in its power.
Mr. Gridley is an old Douglas Democrat, and, although acting with the Copperhead party, his honor and devotion to the humane effort of relieving the sick and wounded soldier are undoubted by those who know him

best. He received from the officers of the Sanitary Fund of this city the very highest testimonials, which alone should have satisfied the editor of the *Star*, had he the real interest of the Fund at heart. Why any paper of the pretensions of the *Star* should attempt to cast a chill upon so noble an object as that in which Mr. Gridley is engaged, is more than we can conceive.

Mr. Gridley is a merchant of wealth and of the highest respectability of this city. Here is his property and here his family resides, and here, among his many friends of either party, the shameful insinuation of the "Query" will be received with the indignation it deserves.

Two days later, on May 31, the *Reveille* returned to the defense of the town's best publicized citizens by pointing out that the entire sum raised by the auction had been used to purchase silver produced by the Reese River mines, and that the latter, in five heavy bricks, had already been "forwarded by officers of the Sanitary Fund to their proper destination." Then, by way of a parting shot at the Sacramento paper, the editor observed ironically: "Mr. Gridley would not make as good time running off with a ton and a half of silver bricks as he did in carrying his sack of flour through the streets of Austin."

Meantime, those serving on Sanitary Fund committees in other western towns had not been slow to recognize that the Reese River flour was a highly effectual money-raising device, and soon requests began flowing into Austin asking that Gridley bring his historic sack to other communities and conduct auctions there. This the doughty grocer was quite willing to do. The result was that for the next several months his fellow townsmen saw little of him, although frequent stories in the columns of the *Reveille* permitted them to keep fairly close tab on his activities.

Logically enough, the place where the perambulating sack and its keeper first made guest appearances was the Comstock Lode, some one hundred eighty miles to the west, the towns of which — Virginia City, Gold Hill, and Silver City — were sustained by the richest group of mines in the Territory. Of their reception on the Lode, the Gold Hill *Daily News*, which had earlier been unimpressed by the Austin auction, gave this account on May 17:

Yesterday was a great day for the wandering Flour Sack of Reese. After having been sold, re-donated and resold in Austin until the proceeds amounted to the noble sum of $5,300, it has been brought to Virginia [City] where, on Sunday, it was again sold for the sum of $580. Yesterday with great pomp and waving banners and martial music it arrived at Gold Hill . . .

The Sack arrived at a propitious moment, stopped in front of the Bank Exchange, just as our Extra was issued announcing the important and cheering news of the victorious onward march of our armies under Grant and Thomas and Schofield. The news was read from the carriage to the assembled multitude. Thomas Fitch addressed the people, announcing the arrival and giving the past history of the wonderful Flour Sack. The bidding then commenced, and at its close reached the magnificent sum of $6,052.50.

From hence the procession moved forward to Silver City and Dayton. At the former place $895 was received, and at the latter, $1,299. Returning through Gold Hill it again stopped and further bidding took place until the whole amount contributed by Gold Hill footed up to nearly $7,000. In the evening, at Virginia, the stores of L. Fusler & Co. and Gillig, Mott & Co. were illuminated; speeches were made and the bidding amounted to $12,-025. With three rousing cheers for U. S. Grant, the meeting adjourned.

In Virginia City, the chief town of the Lode, the auction was held on the evening of May 16, during which, according to one account, "C Street, at the intersection of Taylor, was completely blocked with an immense and excited crowd." The cheers that greeted each bid were said to have "echoed through the city like the voice of many waters, attracting people from all directions." The amount raised there exceeded thirteen thousand dollars — which led one reporter to comment that the Austin flour must be of the "self-rising" variety.

The Austinites were, of course, by no means indifferent to the acclaim with which the local grocer and his flour were being received elsewhere, and the *Reveille* did its best to keep them informed. On May 24, a long editorial, entitled "That Sack of Flour," pointed out that "mighty changes in the tide of human affairs often hinge on the most trivial circumstances," and hazarded the guess that the simple election bet might have set in motion a great humanitarian movement that would bring lasting fame and honor to the town. Having recalled the result of the impromptu auction, the writer went on:

We thought this was doing well, very well, for a young community like this; one which had spent more than a million dollars in one short year in building their houses in this almost desert land, with its silver oasis. Yet the flour sack is scarcely started on its journey, in care of its original owner, when the loyal and liberal citizens of Storey and Lyon counties take the Sanitary contagion in its most hopeful form and relieve themselves by a glorious contribution of over twenty-three thousand dollars: Austin is outdone, but yet has the honor of starting the good work and contributing her mite.

Where will this now famous sack of flour reach its first cold rebuff? Not this side of Dixie we hope. We shall presently expect our faithful and loyal neighbors in California to meet it with purses wide open and that it will go East and come West through the states to St. Louis, gathering the essential oil of human kindness in its tangible form — cash — until a million dollars may be added. . . .

En passant, we may say that it will be a curious fact in the history of Austin that last year St. Louis flour freighted across the plains sold here at four dollars for fifty pounds, and now we send a sack to that city, which has already realized nearly $30,000.

Having successfully toured the Comstock towns in late May, Gridley continued on west in response to urgent appeals from California. The *Reveille* on June 1 informed its readers that their townsman and his much-sold flour had appeared the evening before at the Metropolitan Theater in San Francisco, where Dr. Bellows, head of the Sanitary Commission in California, had delivered an eloquent address from the stage, and Jerome Rice had served as auctioneer. Next day this brief item appeared:

We are pleased to learn that our esteemed friend and fellow citizen Gridley, at the recent sale of the Sanitary Sack at the Metropolitan Theater in San Francisco, arose and firmly repudiated the insinuations against his loyalty. He was enthusiastically cheered and retired amidst overwhelming applause.

On June 7, the San Francisco papers containing stories of the auction there having reached Austin, the *Reveille* printed additional details, culled from the San Francisco *Bulletin's* account.

The object [stated the *Bulletin*], trimmed in red, white and blue ribbons, and labeled in bold letters "Gridley Sanitary Sack," was placed upon a small table in the middle distance of the stage — the table being elevated on a platform. At either side of it sat Mr. Gridley, the owner, Jerome Rice, the auctioneer, R. G. March, one of the proprietors of the Metropolitan, several of the actors [who had earlier appeared in a comedy called *Love and Champagne*], and Charles L. Wiggin, the Mayor's Clerk. . . .

Wiggin said the sack had so far raised $50,000 and that Mr. Girdley intends to take it East and hopes to realize as much as half a million dollars from its sale. . . . Mr. Gridley then gave the history of the sack. He stated that it was A-1 in quality and was manufactured by John Bidwell, the pioneer of Butte County, who had gone east as one of our delegates to the Baltimore Convention. Mr. Gridley denied earnestly the aspersions that have been cast upon his loyalty by one or two prints, and stated that he had fought under the flag for two years in Mexico and had never done, and would never do, anything to disgrace it. . . .

The enthusiastic audience pelted the stage with silver coins — a grateful but dangerous shower. . . .

A short item in the *Reveille* for June 6 reveals that Gridley had returned to Austin the previous day from what the paper termed his "triumphal tour." His stay was brief, however, for he was soon on the road again, this time on an extended trip that carried him, via Panama, to the Atlantic Coast, and thence westward again as far as St. Louis. The local paper, of course, kept close tab on the town's most celebrated citizen during his travels. On the whole, however, it was not much impressed by the treatment he was receiving in the eastern press. Thus, on February 11, 1865, appeared this item:

R. C. Gridley, Esq., of this city, has not only got into New York, but also got into the papers, bag and baggage. *Harper's Weekly* for January 21st has an engraving purporting to be a picture of Gridley and his famous Sanitary Flour. Looking at the engraving, we are at a loss to tell which is Gridley and which is the sack of flour; but go to Frank Drake's, buy the paper, and you can have your choice. We remember our fellow-townsman as a rather handsome man, but this has no more resemblance to Gridley "than I to Hercules."

Probably because by the time of his arrival in New York the Civil War was nearing its close, the auctions aroused far less interest there than they had on the Pacific coast, and thus proved a less effectual means of raising money for the Fund. Nonetheless Gridley — who, as he had done from the beginning, continued to pay his own expenses — proceeded westward according to plan, making a number of stops en route and, after having seen his famous sack auctioned at the Fund's climactic fair at St. Louis, returned overland to Austin.

III

ALTHOUGH during the nine months since he had paid off his election bet, Gridley had been instrumental in raising a very substantial sum — the total was variously estimated at from one hundred thousand dollars to two hundred seventy-five thousand dollars — for the cause, and in so doing had earned for himself the title of "distinguished humanitarian" and been pronounced "one of the greatest unarmed heroes of the war," it presently developed that these honors had been won at heavy cost. For he returned to Austin not only heavily in debt but broken in health. His grocery store at the corner of Water and Second streets, which had been one of the leading mercantile houses of the town, had been steadily losing ground during his absence. His three partners, W. W. Hobart, and Henry and Julius Jacobs, had all withdrawn, and soon after his return he took in a new partner, the firm becoming Gridley & Callow. Meantime, the end of the war had brought a sharp drop in the price of silver; a majority of the Reese River mines had shut down — many never to reopen — and as a consequence Austin itself went into a profound decline.

The result was that he remained in the town, which he had done so much to make known to the nation, only about a year after his return from the east. The Austin City Directory for 1866, the only one ever published, listed him and his partner as "Retail Dealers in Groceries and Provisions." In the fall of that year, however, his failing health having made it inadvisable to pass another winter in the high altitude of the mining town, he moved to California, settling first at Stockton and later at the village of Paradise in Stanislaus County. There he opened a grocery store which he conducted until his death on November 24, 1870.

Oddly enough, although but six years had passed since Gridley and his flour had been universally regarded as Austin's most conspicuous and celebrated ornaments, so quickly was he forgotten that on his death in nearby California no mention of his passing appeared in the columns of the *Reveille*. However, events were to prove that his memory, while temporarily in eclipse, was soon to be restored to something approaching its old place. Chief credit for this revival belongs to another temporary resident of the state, Mark Twain, who in *Roughing It*, published in 1872, devoted a chapter to Gridley and his labors on behalf of the Fund.

Twain's knowledge of the other's exploit sprang from two circumstances, either of which would have assured his interest. One was that the two men were friends of long standing, both having come from Hannibal, Missouri, and having, Twain stated, been schoolmates there. Secondly, during the period in 1864 when the Austin grocer suddenly leaped into national prominence, Twain was laying the foundations of a greater and more lasting fame as a reporter on the *Territorial Enterprise* at Virginia City.

Hence, when Gridley and his flour reached the Comstock in May of 1864, one may be sure that Twain was on hand to welcome the new arrival, appearing not only in his professional capacity but out of a friendly desire to greet another ex-resident of the Missouri town. That Twain was one of the reporters who covered Gridley's visit is clear from a reference to the journalist in an account of the ceremonies at Gold Hill published in that town's *Daily News* for May 16. After describing the cavalcade that convoyed the sack over the divide from Virginia City, the Gold Hill writer, with the frankness characteristic of the Comstock's uninhibited journalism, added this note:

"Tone" was given to the procession by the presence of "Gov." Twain and his staff of bibulous reporters, who came down in a free carriage, ostensibly for the purpose of making notes, but in reality in the pursuit of free whisky.

Twain's version of the adventure in *Roughing It* differs widely from that published in the *Reveille* and other Nevada papers of the time. This was perhaps partly due to the fact that some half-dozen years had passed before he wrote the story and his faulty memory may have caused him to slip up on some of the details. A more likely explanation, however, is that the humorist, as was his custom, took certain liberties with the facts in order to make a better story. Thus, his account of how it all began starts off in this fashion:

A former schoolmate of mine, by the name of Reuel Gridley, was living in the little city of Austin, in the Reese River country, at the time, and was the Democratic candidate for mayor. He and the Republican candidate made an agreement that the defeated man should be publicly presented with a fifty-pound sack of flour by the successful one, and should carry it home on his shoulder. Gridley was defeated. The new mayor gave him the sack of flour, and he shouldered it and carried it a mile or two from Lower Austin to his home in Upper Austin, attended by a band of music and the whole population. Arrived there, he said he did not need the flour, and asked what the people thought he had better do with it. A voice said:

"Sell it to the highest bidder, for the benefit of the Sanitary fund."

Gridley forthwith mounted a drygoods box, Twain goes on, and called for bids, which were made with great liberality by the crowd. "So Gridley stood there," he continues, "and shouted and perspired until the sun went down; and when the crowd dispersed he had sold the sack to three hundred different people, and taken in eight thousand dollars in gold. . . ."

Twain adds that when news of this exploit reached Virginia City, officials there promptly dispatched a telegram to Austin reading: "Fetch along your flour sack!" The result was that thirty-six hours later Gridley reached town, and a series of auctions followed in the various Comstock towns, which netted a total of some forty thousand dollars, the climax being reached at Virginia City, the inhabitants of which contributed "in the neighborhood of three dollars for each man, woman and child of the population. It was," he concludes, "the greatest day Virginia ever saw. . . ."

The *Roughing It* account states that Gridley later took the sack to San Francisco and from there to the East Coast, winding up at St. Louis, "where a monster Sanitary Fair was being held." Twain then adds a probably imaginary but highly appropriate touch: that "after selling it for a large sum and helping on the enthusiasm by displaying the portly silver bricks which Nevada's donations had produced, he had the flour baked into small cakes and retailed at high prices."

A less fanciful but better substantiated version of what finally happened to the historic bag of flour is that, after his barnstorming tour through the east, Gridley carried it back with him to Austin, and that, many years later, it found its way into the museum of the Nevada Historical Society at Reno, where it is now one of the Society's prize exhibits.

Gridley's subsequent history can be briefly told. "He returned in 1865 from his trip East to find his business dwindled to small proportions and himself financially ruined," stated the Stockton *Independent* some years later. "He came to Stockton in 1866, without a dollar, having been brought over the mountains in the bed of a wagon." With his wife and four children he settled in the California town. The hoped-for improvement in his health, however, failed to materialize, and some months later word drifted back to Austin that he and his family were in dire straits. On January 3, 1867, the *Reveille* printed a letter from an Austin mine manager, Major A. E. Sherman, who had served with Gridley in the Mexican War, in which he inquired: "Shall it be said that R. C.

Gridley, his wife and little ones, shall suffer, so long as there remains a man in Austin to divide with him his last dollar? I trust not!"

That the letter-writer was correct in his surmise is clear from the fact that on January 10 the *Reveille* devoted a long article to a resumé of the ex-townsman's services to the Sanitary Fund and his part in making the town known throughout the nation. "This," the story went on, "is the history of Mr. Gridley's days of health and vigor. But his condition is changed; he is now prostrated by sickness . . . needing care and attention." The story ended in the announcement that Major Sherman would deliver a lecture on the evening of January 16; his subject to be the Mexican War and the proceeds to go to the ill man.

In the same issue of the paper was an interview with Dave Buel, the defeated candidate for mayor in the election that had projected Gridley into national prominence. "Make him well," announced Buel, "and then we'll build him a little house and bring him here to live with us. . . ."

At Major Sherman's lecture the Methodist Church was crowded to capacity, and at its conclusion a number of speeches in praise of the ailing man were delivered, "following which the audience . . . one by one came forward and put their contributions on the table." On January 18, the local paper thus reported the result: "Total amount collected, $713.25; total expenses, $20; net amount sent Gridley, $693.25.

Buel's proposal that Gridley be brought back to live in Austin was never carried out. Instead, as we have seen, he moved with his family to the foothill village of Para-

dise and there opened a grocery store, presumably with
the funds raised at the Austin lecture, and there he remained until his death in 1870.

He was buried at Stockton where, for more than a decade, his body lay in an unmarked grave, the world having
seemingly forgotten his brief season of fame. But that was
not to be. In the summer of 1882, the Stockton Post of
the Grand Army of the Republic interested itself in the
matter and launched a campaign to raise funds to put up
a fitting marker. As a means of furthering that project,
the G.A.R. issued a forty-page pamphlet "Compiled and
published for the purpose of raising money to aid in the
building of a monument to his memory, and establishing
a fund for his family." The text of this work related again
the story of the Sanitary Fund and the historic flour sack.
The back page reproduced a woodcut of the monument it
was proposed to erect on his grave: a life-sized statue
of the humanitarian standing atop a marble pedestal, his
figure clad in a frock coat, one hand thrust inside the
breast of the coat, the other resting on the sack, across the
front of which were engraved the words: "Austin Sanitary
Flour."

The Rawlins Post of the G.A.R., the sponsors of this enterprise, carried on with so much zeal that the necessary
funds were promptly raised. The statue of the hero,
"carved from choicest Carrara marble and standing 6 feet
10 inches high," together with its marble base, were ordered from Italy. Some five years later, on September 9,
1887 — California's Admission Day — residents of Stockton watched the G.A.R. veterans parade through the down-
town streets, then followed the brass bands out to the
cemetery. There they listened to an oration in Gridley's

praise by a local judge, and at its conclusion cheered lustily as the curtains were drawn aside and the heroic figure stood revealed.

Ironically, this unveiling of this memorial seems to have stirred no interest in the little Reese River town where Reuel Gridley's rocketlike rise to fame had begun, for the file of the local paper for the month of September 1887 contains no word of the event. For once the *Reveille's* keen-eyed editor had been caught napping.

CHAPTER FIVE

The Odyssey of Charles Breyfogle

I

THE discovery of rich ledges in Pony Canyon in the fall of 1862 attracted to the Reese River country not only hundreds of practical miners intent on developing the new claims, locating others, and building mills for the reduction of the ores, but, close on their heels, came a numerous group of men of quite another stamp. These were the speculators, shrewd operators whose sole aim was to exploit the nationwide interest in the new discoveries by staking out claims — almost any claim would do — organizing companies bearing confidence-inspiring names, and reaping quick profits by the sale of stock on the exchanges in Virginia City, San Francisco, and the cities of the east.

The avidity with which the public on both coasts, as well as in London and other European cities, invested in these fly-by-night properties, the great majority of which were barren of millable ore, was long a source of wonderment to the residents of Austin and other Nevada mining towns. Charles Allen, a Bostonian who visited the Reese River camps in 1865, in a letter published in the *Springfield Republican,* wrote that: "A leading citizen of this place [Austin] remarked to me: 'I do not see why eastern gentlemen who have surplus funds will invest them in our mines, while there are faro banks at home.' "

In that same year, J. Ross Browne, following his weeks-long survey of the region, stated that he "must have read a dozen pamphlets devoted to enthusiastic descriptions of mining properties purchased by New York companies, which to the best of my belief exist only on paper." He went on to express his surprise that so many normally hard-headed businessmen persisted in investing their funds in such enterprises after only the most casual of investigations, and frequently after none at all.

Is it any wonder then [he concluded] that when the grand purchase is consummated, superintendents and experts appointed, machinery shipped, and everything is under way to develop the vast resources of the company's possessions, that the five hundred ledges are found to be merely conjectural, the forty thousand acres of woodland a patch of scrubby pines in some inaccessible mountain region, the hundred mill-sites scattered over a sage-desert where there is not water enough to run a grindstone, and the twenty-five town-sites agreeably situated in the middle of an alkali lake!

With evidences of the credulity of distant investors visible on every side, it is not surprising that Austin's opportunists made haste to get aboard the gravy train. In fact, they went into the business on so lavish a scale that before the town was two years old the number of duly incorporated Reese River mining and milling companies exceeded six thousand. So numerous did these stock-

selling schemes become that in the spring of 1865 the
Reveille was moved to protest, its editor pointing out that
they were giving the region a bad name among monied
men all over the country and making it increasingly difficult to finance the development of legitimate mines, mills,
and other enterprises. This warning, of course, went unheeded and projects of that sort continued to be launched
until, as the editor wryly remarked two years later, "the
well finally ran dry."

Not all such undertakings were directly concerned with
mining. Stage and freight companies, irrigation projects,
farming and stock-raising colonies, water works, and numerous others were organized and their stock offered to
investors anxious to share in the profits of the new bonanza. One such was so ingenious that it became a permanent part of the annals of the town, its story remembered and pridefully repeated even today. This was the
Reese River Navigation Company, the purpose of which,
according to its sponsors, was to cut the cost of transporting ore in wagons from the area's widely scattered mines to
the Austin mills by loading it on barges and towing them
down the Reese River. The company's stock found a ready
sale in New York, Boston, and elsewhere in the east,
where the investors were blissfully unaware that for nine
months of the year the Reese River was completely dry
and even in the wet season rarely had more than a few
inches of water in its sandy bed.

A traveler in the mid-1860's gives this account of his
first encounter with that mighty stream. Their stage having, he states, spent two days and a night passing over
a completely parched and barren desert country, during
the second night "our driver cracks his whip, and our

stage makes a dive into a little rut and out again. There is a faint show of water on the wheels."

"What's that?" cries everybody in amazement.

"Gents," says the driver, "I don't want to alarm you; but that's Reese River."

Still remembered is another Austin speculation which financed the building of what remains to this day one of the town's chief architectural ornaments. In 1864, a group of citizens belonging to the Methodist faith launched a campaign to raise funds for a place of worship in keeping with the growing importance of the town. In addition to cash, so many mining shares were donated that the committee in charge shrewdly pooled their holdings, organized the Methodist Mining Company, and offered stock for sale. The result exceeded their fondest hopes. One version states that the sum raised was close to a quarter of a million dollars, and the impressive brick structure that presently arose was for many years pointed out as the handsomest church in Nevada.

A year or two earlier during yet another fund-raising drive, a somewhat similar scheme was employed. During the early months of 1863, the women of Austin had, as stated earlier, taken the lead in a campaign to provide a proper building to house the town's school. While the drive was in progress, a group of local men decided to do their bit. Accordingly, one of their number conceived the plan of getting possession of a pair of boots belonging to Dave Buel, a man of unusually large stature, whose boots were locally celebrated because of their prodigious size, and auctioning them off for the benefit of the school fund. This he succeeded in doing and from a stand set up on Main Street the auction got under way.

Each time they were knocked down to the highest bidder the new owner presented them again to the auctioneer and the sale went on. By the time the fun was over and the boots returned to their original owner, one hundred six dollars had been raised.

II

THE discovery of the rich Reese River ledges, however, attracted not only its quota of promoters and speculators but a considerable group of miners of another class. These were the authentic prospectors, a distinct species of pioneer who had been familiar on the western frontier since the beginnings of the California gold rush a dozen years earlier. Of that picturesque breed, J. Ross Browne wrote in 1865:

The prospector is a man of imagination. He is a poet — though not generally aware of the fact. Ragged and unshaved, he owns millions, yet seldom has two dimes to jingle in his pocket — for his wealth lies in the undeveloped wilds. The spirit of unrest burns in his blood. He scorns work, but will endure any amount of hardship in his endless search for "rich leads." There is no desert too barren, no climate too rigorous for his researches. From the rugged canyon of the Toiyabe he roams to the arid base of the Great Basin. Hunger, thirst, chilling snows, and scorching sands seem to give him new life and inspiration. It matters nothing that he discovers a "good thing" — a nest of ledges, worth say a million apiece — this is well enough, but he wants something better; and after a day or two spent in "locating his claims" he is off again — nobody knows where — often with scarcely provisions enough to last him back to the settlements. He travels on mule-back, when he happens to own a mule; on foot when he must; with company, when any offers; without, when there is none; any way to be driving ahead, discovering new regions and locating claims. He locates so many claims that he forgets where his possessions are. If he discovered a ledge of pure silver, six feet deep, he would die in a week if he had to work it on his own account. Variety is the spice of his existence, the motive-power of his life. . . .

Using the new camp as a base of supplies, the prospectors were presently setting off on treks during which they explored the countless steep canyons and gullies of central Nevada's arid mountain ranges. During the course of the next few years, these solitary desert rats located dozens of ledges promising enough to attract a quota of followers and bring about the establishment of new camps, some to be abandoned after a few weeks or months, others to remain active for years.

Among Austin's prospectors there were, however, a few whose quest for mineral riches carried them much further afield. One such was a man whose wanderings were to give him a degree of fame and win him a permanent place in western history and folklore. This was Charles C. Breyfogle, an Ohioan who had emigrated to California during the gold rush, settled down in Oakland where he for several years served as an Alameda County official, and then, as the decade of the 1850's ended, joined in the stampede across the Sierra to the Comstock Lode. Three years later, he was in the van of the new rush to the Reese River where, by the spring of 1864, he was operating a hotel at Geneva, an attractively located mountain settlement a dozen miles to the east of Austin, his wanderings seemingly over.

But it presently grew clear that Breyfogle was still a prospector at heart. Just what was the impulse that set him off on the trail again is not clear, but it is evident that the wanderlust was in his blood and if it had not been one thing it would have been another. All that is known is that some time in 1864 he assembled an outfit, loaded a pack-mule with supplies for a long journey, and headed south from Geneva, down the Big Smoky Valley. One theory is that during his stay in California he had heard from other '49ers, who had come west via the Death Valley route, tales of fantastically rich ledges they had stumbled on there but which in their desperate plight — being without food or water — they had had to abandon in order to push on westward at all possible speed.

Some who have attempted to reconstruct the story of Breyfogle's wanderings theorize that these Death Valley pioneers had given him information which he believed would enable him to find one of the lost ledges. In any event, he journeyed southward into the arid country to the east of the Funeral Mountains. There, at Ash Meadows — one of the few water holes in the region — he seems to have joined forces with several others and with them continued on toward the southwest, skirting the southern border of Death Valley and presumably headed for San Bernardino. Somewhere along the route, however, the party was set on by a band of Piutes; his companions were slain and Breyfogle himself barely managed to escape, leaving behind nearly all his possessions. Without food, weapons, and — most serious of all — water, he fled northward toward the most desolate and forbidding part of the Valley.

His wanderings during the weeks that followed constitute one of the most remarkable — and puzzling — sagas of the pioneer west. Toward the close of the first day, he, according to his later account, stumbled on a depression filled with brackish water, heavily impregnated with salt, which he called Coyote Holes. Filling his shoes, the only receptacles he possessed, with the evil-tasting liquid, he pushed on, slept a few hours and, at the first hint of dawn, continued toward the northeast. During the second day, or perhaps the third — the passage of time had already grown hazy in his mind — he spied in the distance a belt of green vegetation that held promise of what he most desperately needed: water. When, however, after hours of effort, he reached the area, his hopes were dashed; the green patch proved to be gnarled mesquite shrubs devoid of moisture.

It was either while he was struggling up the mountainside toward that spot, or making his painful way back down to the valley's floor, that the wanderer made a discovery that was to haunt his dreams for the balance of his life — and, incidentally, to stir the imagination of treasure-hunters from that day down to the present. For somewhere in the vicinity of the mesquite-covered mountainside, his route took him over an intervening ridge, the sides of which were composed of a reddish soil from which protruded an outcropping of rock. Even in the dire straits in which he found himself, his prospecting instincts were still strong enough to cause him to pick up a fragment of the brittle quartz. This specimen, and those all about, were heavily infused with gold; it was ore vastly richer than any he had ever laid eyes on.

In his extremity, he could not tarry long on the spot; however, he gathered up a few fragments, tied them in a handkerchief, and then pushed on. Then followed the most amazing part of his entire odyssey. Trudging onward at night so as to avoid the killing heat of the Death Valley summer, and laying his course northward by means of the stars, he made his way, during the period that followed, which must have occupied two weeks or longer, through the rugged wastes of the Valley, across the arid plains to the north (where the towns of Tonopah and Goldfield were later to rise), and was eventually discovered by a passing rancher roaming on the sagebrush in the vicinity of Round Mountain at the edge of the Toquima Range and only about forty miles from Austin. He had covered a distance of some two hundred miles, subsisting on whatever he could get his hands on, tormented by thirst, with his body covered with bruises and his mind clouded. Yet through it all he had grimly held on to the little bundle of golden quartz he had picked up near the beginning of his rovings.

III

AT FIRST sight, it seems strange that Breyfogle's perilous adventure and his all but miraculous survival — to say nothing of the startlingly rich ores he had brought with him out of the unknown — should have aroused hardly a ripple of interest in Austin, the town to which he was taken by his rescuer and where he spent the weeks of his convalescence. Yet the files of the *Reveille* during the summer and fall of 1864 contain no reference at all to this resident of the neighboring village of Geneva or the fearsome ordeal through which he had passed. It seems hardly likely that the paper's editor, usually so alert to gather in every scrap of local news, had missed this episode entirely and so passed up one of the most dramatic human interest stories the area had ever known. The answer may be that Breyfogle himself, together with the two or three men with whom he shared his secret, had taken extraordinary pains to keep the matter quiet, and in that attempt had succeeded far better than is usually the case. Yet another possibility is that the editor, having learned of Breyfogle's asserted discovery, decided to make no mention of it, foreseeing what effect its publication would have.

For those in on the news, there was indeed every reason to keep it from the public at large. For soon after he was brought to Austin, Breyfogle's carefully hoarded ore specimens had been taken to a local assayer, one Jacob Gooding, and they proved, as Gooding stated later, extremely rich, some of them being half pure gold, and the whole assaying at what he estimated to be in the neighborhood of one hundred thousand dollars per ton. Assuming that the *Reveille's* editor was one of the limited group that shared this information, it is not difficult to picture the dilemma facing him. The ore was of a value unprecedented in western mining history. To spread abroad news of its discovery would inevitably have set in motion a stampede that in numbers and urgency would have surpassed all previous rushes.

Nor is it hard to envision what the effect would have been on the fortunes of Austin and its adjacent camps. The town was then at the height of its boom, with its mines and mills just getting into full production, with its population growing, employment high, and all — merchants, mine and mill owners, and the *Reveille* itself — enjoying high prosperity. It was clear that to publicize Breyfogle's sensational find, and thus send hundreds of local residents off on a concerted rush to the south, could not fail to have a disastrous effect on the town. Hence, it is well within the realm of possibility that had the editor learned of the prospector's find, he prudently agreed to co-operate in efforts to keep the discovery secret.

Breyfogle himself and the small group of local residents in whom he had confided were meantime laying plans to hurry down to the fabulous red hill and stake out their claims. They impatiently awaited the time when the exhausted man would be well enough to travel again, meantime obsessed by the fear that others might stumble on the ledge. The party unobtrusively left Austin in the fall of 1864, but upon reaching the lower edge of Death Valley were prevented from proceeding farther northward by the presence of strong bands of warlike Piutes. Temporarily abandoning their quest, the disappointed party returned to Austin.

In the spring of the following year, however, they set off again and this time succeeded in locating Coyote Holes, the shallow bodies of salty water Breyfogle had stumbled on while fleeing from the Indians months before. Success then seemed near, for Breyfogle had no doubt that from that point he could retrace his steps and lead the party to the treasure. It was, he asserted, necessary only to locate the clump of mesquite shrubs toward which he had hurried after leaving Coyote Holes; the outcropping of golden quartz was close by.

But now unlooked-for difficulties arose. The mesquite, having meantime shed its leaves, was no longer visible as a patch of green, and, although there were many reddish-colored hills in the region, all those the group examined proved barren. As the fruitless search continued for days and weeks, the high hopes of Breyfogle's companions gradually waned. The other, however, was certain that he would eventually get his bearings, and the hunt continued, taking in an ever-widening area, following the northeasterly course he was presumed to have taken on his long trek through the Valley.

In the course of their travels, the group came on a second party of Austin prospectors who were looking for yet another lost claim. This was a rich deposit of silver said to have been discovered by a company of California emigrants known as the Jayhawkers while crossing the Valley early in 1850, and known as the Lost Gunsight because one of the party had there fashioned a bit of metal into a sight to replace one lost from his rifle. On learning of Breyfogle's golden ledge, members of this party abandoned their own quest and the two groups joined forces. The search continued until, having made their way to the summit of the Funeral Range on the eastern border of the Valley and finding both their hopes and their supplies at a low ebb, the disappointed group gave up the search and returned to Austin. All, that is, except Breyfogle; he remained behind, still determined to relocate the fabulous ledge.

Here, as in many other phases of the Breyfogle saga, two versions of what happened have been preserved. One states that he was summarily abandoned by his companions; another that he was left a plentiful supply of provisions and that the others promised to return later and take up the search again. It is this latter version that found its way into print in the columns of the *Reveille* when the group reached Austin in late April. After telling of the adventures of the Lost Gunsight party during their two months of wandering in the Valley, the story, dated April 24, 1865, concludes with this paragraph:

Previously they had fallen in with a party from Smoky Valley composed of Messrs. Breyfogle, E. T. Martin, A. A. Simondson, G. W. Cloud and McKinistry. There they were in quest of some gold-bearing quartz lodes that Mr. Breyfogle had found on a previous expedition. The precise nature of what that company found was not disclosed, but it is sufficient to induce them to return. Mr. Breyfogle was left two months supplies of provisions to hold the place and prospect during the absence of the others.

Something of the nature of Breyfogle's find must have become generally known by then, for the account concludes with this ironical comment: "We expect shortly to hear of a far richer district than is even Reese River. . . ."

Two other items in the *Reveille* during the weeks that followed reflect the skepticism with which the paper viewed this hunt for supposedly rich Death Valley ledges.

Thus, on June 10, 1865, it published this paragraph, heading it "They Didn't Find It":

Messrs. Marshal and Gillan have returned from their prospecting tour in quest of a "big thing," minus two of their three animals. They traveled about two hundred miles in a southwesterly direction. In our opinion it would be far pleasanter, and fully as profitable, for those who are inclined for adventure in the search after "lost mines" and "secret treasures" to sit down quietly and read the "Thousand and One Nights." But 'tis distance that lends enchantment to the view.

Three days later, on June 13, the *Reveille* reprinted an article from the Salt Lake *Telegraph* of June 9, indicating that Breyfogle's second stay in Death Valley had been fully as eventful as his first. The story, an interview with a prospector just arrived at Salt Lake from the southwest, concludes with these words:

Mr. Granger tells us that Mr. Breyfogle, of Reese River, who is no doubt also reported dead, is traveling by [wagon] train to Salt Lake. . . . Mr. Granger found Mr. Breyfogle at Las Vegas springs, with two shots in his body and half scalped. He had left his company at Death Valley — very significant — in search of a silver mine, and fell into the hands of a few Indians, who very nigh closed the chronicles of his earthly pilgrimage. . . .

Charles Breyfogle, however, was obviously not one to be turned aside from his objective by such minor mishaps. If, as presently grew clear, his golden ledge was to join the lengthy list of western lost mines, it was no fault of its doughty discoverer. For during the remaining years of his life — he is said to have lived until 1870 — he made repeated journeys into the rugged, waterless reaches of the Valley, sometimes alone, sometimes at the head of well-equipped parties, convinced to the end that success would eventually crown his efforts.

All in vain; the ledge proved permanently elusive, and remains so to the present day. As time passed, it came to be widely believed among experienced mining men that the fabulously rich outcropping had existed only in Breyfogle's imagination; that the strain and privations he had endured on his long flight across the desert had clouded his mind and made him the victim of gaudy hallucinations. Those who have held that view, though, have found it difficult to account for the fact that when the prospector emerged from his ordeal, he carried with him a little horde of gold-bearing quartz and that when these were assayed they proved to be of surpassing rich-ness. The question of where and how he came into pos-session of them was unanswered during his lifetime and has remained a mystery ever since.

CHAPTER SIX

The Sybarites of Pony Canyon

I

DURING much of its history, Austin, contrary to tradition and unlike most western mining towns, was normally a quiet, law-abiding community. Even during the period of its first and last great boom, when Pony Canyon echoed day and night with the sound of boot-clad feet on the board sidewalks, and the screech of saws and thud of hammers as shelters of all sorts were rushed to completion, interspersed with the blaring of the fiddle or accordion and the clink of coins in its numerous open-front gambling houses, even in that turbulent pioneer era, shootings, robberies, and other forms of violence were comparatively rare.

That the *Reveille's* editor — again unlike most of his Nevada contemporaries — was often hard pressed for local crime stories is indicated by the yarn that follows. Soon after the town was incorporated, members of the City Council passed an ordinance requiring dog-owners to buy licenses for their animals and instructing the town marshal to round up all untagged dogs and confine them in the pound. That official, whom the *Reveille* referred to as "mine host of the Hotel de Tray," proceeded to carry out these instructions. Further developments were thus recorded in the issue for January 16, 1865:

JAIL BREAK. — Our city was thrown into a foment of excitement and consternation yesterday morning upon learning that the lawless characters (73 in number), whom Marshal Bodrow had been busy arresting during the past week, had broke jail on the preceding night. The Marshal visited his prisoners in the evening, and after a close scrutiny of the premises, retired, having no suspicion that an escape was contemplated.

Upon an investigation yesterday morning, it was discovered that the prisoners were liberated by friends and accomplices on the outside, who had forced the door. Parties were seen prowling around during the day, and are suspected of having a hand in the business, as they are known to be associates of the culprits. We met the Marshal at the International [hotel] last night, and he appeared heart-broken at the disaster. He underwent an examination before Judge Beatty, and that gentleman is perfectly satisfied that the Marshal had no complicity in the affair. Sheriff Leffingwell and all available police of the city have been in pursuit and, we are happy to state, have recovered quite a number of the dogs.

Such law-breaking and violence as occurred was rarely of a very serious nature, and the *Reveille's* accounts of these occasional infractions were models of brevity. Thus, on May 27, 1864, appeared this item, typical of a number of others:

Night before last two of the prisoners in the county jail relieved the monotony of prison life by a bit of scrimmage, with none to act as bottle holder. The lack of an appreciative audience caused the jailor to interfere, and the fight stopped without serious damage. The cause of the difficulty was said to be a frail — and fair — fellow prisoner.

While it was the editor's habit to dismiss the general run of petty crimes and misdemeanors with a line or two of type, when something of a more serious nature took place he gave it adequate, but by no means overfull, treatment, as shown by the following, from the issue of October 14, 1863:

MAN KILLED. — Reuben Martin, a native of Virginia aged about 24 years, was shot by John Spiker about half-past one o'clock Monday morning, under the following circumstances: Martin had been in the habit of occupying the cabin of F. Heldman as a sleeping place, and on Sunday night after the other occupants had retired, Spiker entered and asked permission to lie down on the floor, which was granted him. Martin, who was absent at the time, then came home, considerably under the influence of liquor, and after striking a light and observing someone on the floor beside his bed, commenced abusing him and ordered him to leave, at the same time cocking his revolver and threatening to shoot. Spiker tried to argue the case with him, but finding it useless, left the house, followed by Martin, who commenced firing at Spiker, who returned in like manner. Five shots were exchanged, one of which entered the right breast of the deceased, passing through the lungs and lodging just beneath the skin on the back, which caused death in about twelve hours. Spiker was arrested, examined before Judge Logan, and was acquitted.

Six months later, on April 20, 1864, another exchange of gunfire was reported in less detail, presumably because there had been no fatalities.

A duel was fought this morning between Billy Mulligan and Tom Coleman. Mulligan was the challenging party, weapons, revolvers at ten paces, advancing after first fire. Coleman was wounded slightly in the thigh; also had a finger of the right hand broken. Five shots were fired on each side. No attempt at arrests. Mulligan was uninjured.

On June 8 came this item:

There was a fine little muss early last evening between a party of men immediately back of our office. We could not make head or tail of the matter, but may be able to understand all about it today, as complaints have been formally made against the alleged guilty parties.

Evidently the participants in this "muss" settled their differences out of court, for the next few issues of the paper made no mention of it. Instead, the editor filled his columns of local news with such observations as these:

We observe numerous signs of late, freshly painted, with this strange device: "Liquors 12½ cents." Taking all things into consideration, and the price of freight in particular, we are inclined to think that they who dispense liquors at 12½ cents a glass do so from charitable motives.

168   *The Town That Died Laughing*

DULL. — Judge Logan did not have a single case before him yesterday, nor could we squeeze an item out of Clerk Locke of the District Court.

By the summer of 1864, it had grown clear that, in marked contrast to the feverish activity of a few months earlier, the town had entered the doldrums, with work on its mines and mills at a temporary standstill and, in consequence, business slack in all lines. This having given rise in some quarters to gloomy views of the area's future, the editor was moved to publish this spirited protest:

The croakers have not all left our city yet, but we expect to make the last shipment in a few days. You hear them around the street corners, complaining of the times, and in nine cases out of ten they are persons who have neither energy nor ambition to do anything in any country, and the sooner we get rid of them the better it will be for all concerned. We are getting along as well as any place on the Pacific Coast, and think we have everything to be thankful for and nothing to complain of.

II

THE rapidity with which the town had cast off the crudities and inconveniences of a frontier community and adopted the ways of civilization was a favorite theme of the *Reveille* all during the early years. Its editor lost few opportunities to point out to the rest of the world

that life there was as varied and orderly and decorous
as in towns far older than Austin. Thus, in the issue for
August 29, 1865, he editorialized:

The experience of Americans has led them to believe
that frontier towns, and those beyond the frontiers, far
in the interior of the country, are but the habitations of
desperate adventurers, and of the ignorant and debased
of society. The stranger visiting Austin, looking for such,
is on the alert with pistol ready, but a few days unde-
ceives him, and he is disarmed of both weapons and fears
and becomes a peaceable citizen, as are his neighbors and
those he meets on the streets. Expecting to find only men,
he is surprised at the display of the fairer portion of
creation, and upon Sundays finds the churches and Sunday schools filled with audiences that would seldom be
surpassed in towns of equal size in the East. The fine
business houses and residences of stone, brick and other
materials, with abundant stores of all the necessities and
luxuries of life, with an efficient police and vigilant fire
department, all speak in inviting tones to those having
families in the quiet towns of the old settled States, and
who desire to link their fortunes with the rising State of
Nevada. . . .

More than a year earlier, on May 28, 1864, the editor
had commented on the growing number of facilities for
recreation and cultural improvement available to residents. Having listed the Y.M.C.A., the Odd Fellows, and
Masons, the church services and Sunday schools already
functioning, with others in the planning stage, he went
on to observe:

It is gratifying to strangers coming into a new place to know where they can spend their evenings in the cultivation of the mind, rather than be forced into a public barroom, where a promiscuous assembly is thrown together and the subject-matter of conversation anything but instructive or congenial to his feelings. If we have not our literary clubs, our dramatic halls or public libraries, we are not altogether deprived of intellectual entertainment. . . . Moreover, the time is not far distant when we shall be able to enjoy all the advantages found in the older cities. This is the youngest city on the Pacific slope, and we doubt not that within a period of three years, Austin will rank in importance as the third city on the coast.

Meantime, the town did not allow its lack of a suitable hall to deprive its residents of entertainment when traveling actors, musicians, or other notables chanced to pass that way on journeys to or from the coast. Thus, in the summer of 1864, when thirty-year-old Artemus Ward toured the west, his drolly humorous lectures drew capacity audiences in the prosperous, amusement-starved Nevada silver towns. His route, via the Overland Stage, took him through Austin, and the announcement that he would deliver one of his talks there aroused much enthusiasm.

There being no hall in the town big enough to accommodate the hundreds who wanted to attend, it was decided to hold the lecture in a stone store then under construction on the main street. Because there was no illumination in the unfinished structure, when the appointed hour came Ward himself left the International Hotel carrying a lighted lamp in his hand and, followed by half the population of the town, led the way to the improvised auditorium. The dimly lighted building was crowded to its utmost capacity and the event was voted a tremendous success.

It was, however, not this meeting that made the humorist's stay at Austin memorable. At the conclusion of his talk, he was approached by a delegation of miners who represented themselves as citizens of an outlying camp called Big Creek, which they described as a thriving city, the residents of which were eager to hear his lecture. Ward's manager, a man named Hingston, at first opposed accepting this engagement, for the Indians had recently been on the warpath in that region and he feared trouble. Eventually, however, Hingston's objections were overcome and the next day Ward, accompanied by a contingent from Austin, journeyed to the camp.

The lecture was delivered in the largest building the place boasted, a saloon called the Little America, which Ward later described as having a dirt floor and a roof made of sagebrush. Using the bar as a rostrum, while the barkeeps to his right and left did a brisk business serving drinks to the audience, Ward delivered his talk to an appreciative crowd of a hundred and fifty, who had paid two dollars each for the privilege.

However, soon after setting off on the lonely road back to Austin, Hingston's worst fears were realized. Suddenly a band of men in the habiliments of Piutes, their faces smeared with war paint, sprang from the sagebrush and surrounded the vehicle. Ward and his manager were roughly drawn to the roadside and made to kneel while their captors, in language unintelligible to the victims, loudly debated what was to be done to them. At length, the band's leader, brandishing a knife above Ward's scalp, demanded in halting English to know his identity. "Artemus Ward," replied the shaken lecturer, whereupon his interrogator, in a tone of marked distaste, exclaimed: "Ugh, the talkee man," and commanded him to begin his "talkee." The badly frightened Ward thereupon launched into his lecture, raising his voice higher and higher to make himself heard above the blood-thirsty cries of the others who, in their outlandish tongue, were evidently still debating his fate. Presently, however, he became aware that a change had come over his captors; their attitude was no longer menacing; instead, they were standing about, convulsed with laughter.

Not until then did Ward realize that he had been made the butt of a typical mining-camp hoax; that his tormentors were Austin miners masquerading as Indians. The party thereupon continued on to town and repaired to a bar, where the humorist bought drinks for the crowd and joined in their merriment over his unscheduled road-side lecture.

The lack of entertainment was sorely felt all during the first year or two and such traveling artists who appeared there were assured of capacity audiences. The first of these appears to have been a Professor Simmons, billed as "the noted sleight of hand performer," who showed up early in 1863. In reporting the two local exhibitions of his skill, the newly founded *Reveille* commented on January 23: "These 'black art' fellows do some strange things, but Simmons is the first one we ever heard of who indulged in the pastime of cutting his cranium off, and exhibiting his brainless trunk for the

amusement of the audience." On departing eastward, the
Professor stated that he was hurrying to New York where
he had been booked for an important series of engagements.

A few weeks later, on March 8, appeared this announcement, headed "Theatrical Stars Coming":

We are informed by telegraph that Mr. and Mrs.
Irvine, two theatrical stars of note, will arrive in this
place in the course of a few weeks. They are now sojourn-
ing in Salt Lake and propose to play a few evenings in
Austin and vicinity, providing a suitable hall can be obtained.

Evidently the plans of the Irvines miscarried, or it may
have been that no proper hall could be found; at any
rate, the paper during the next month bore no account
of their local appearances. However, the camp was not
without other forms of entertainment, as indicated by
this paragraph on March 12:

Bill David, who is matched for a mill against Patsy
Daley for a $2000 side, will give a grand sparring exhi-
bition to-morrow night, at the Capitol Saloon. He will be
assisted by various notables of the prize ring, and will accommodate any amateur with a friendly set-to who may
wish it. He will no doubt have a large turn-out, and this
will be the only opportunity the public will have to witness the Pacific champion before his fight with Daley.
The price of admission will be one dollar.

A year later, the town was still deploring its lack of
amusements and giving a warm welcome to any profes-

sional entertainers who chanced to come that way. Thus,
on May 10, 1864, the paper reported:

Some prominent theatrical stars from California will
soon pass through here on their way to Salt Lake. Among
them are Charles Pope, Walter Laman, and Miss Virginia Howard. We hope they will come prepared to give
a few representations at this place. We have but poor
buildings for a theater, but in such as we have Artemus
Ward was enabled to make over a thousand dollars by two
lectures. It is long since we have been favored with any
amusement of the kind and think a good company would
do well to make us a visit.

Not until early the following year did the completion
of the Odd Fellows' Hall provide a proper setting for
theatrical performances. In mid-February, 1865, the new
building was fittingly dedicated to the drama by the appearance there of a touring San Francisco company
headed by the Chapmans, a husband and wife team of
actors then celebrated all over the west. Following the
opening on a Saturday night, the play being *Black Eyed
Susan,* the *Reveille,* after stating that the hall had been
filled to its utmost capacity, commented:

The Chapman family are too well known to require
any laudation from our hands, and everybody must go
and see and judge for themselves. Taking into consideration the number of bad colds contracted on the road
hither, the want of scenery, machinery, etc., members of
the company acquitted themselves creditably. . . .

Thereafter, until the completion of the transcontinental railroad in 1869, theatrical troupes passing through on the Overland Stages from time to time made overnight stops at Austin and put on performances for the amusement-starved natives. However, by then, the town's brief period of prosperity had already passed, with most of its mills and mines permanently shut down, and from 1870 onward the diminished population had, for the most part, to depend on home talent to provide their entertainment.

III

THROUGHOUT its entire history, the town's isolation has had a profound effect on the manner of life lived there. Situated as it is near the geographical center of the big, sparsely settled state, and separated by hundreds of miles from the principal markets and sources of supply, the inconveniences and delays and high cost of transporting goods of all sorts to and from the place have always presented a major problem.

The handicap imposed by being so far removed from other populous centers was felt with particular intensity during the first few years. For with population growing by leaps and bounds and each day bringing its sizable quota of new arrivals, the question of how to procure adequate supplies was a formidable one, for virtually none of the necessities — to say nothing of the luxuries — demanded by the inhabitants could be produced locally. Thus, through all of 1863 and much of the next year, transportation facilities were taxed to their utmost, with every sort of conveyance capable of carrying goods across the many miles of barren country that lay to the east and west being pressed into service.

One result of this was the appearance in Austin in the summer of 1864 of a species of pack animals which a majority of the residents had never before laid eyes on. In its issue for August 26, the *Reveille* thus heralded the advent of this novelty:

SHIPS OF THE DESERT. — A train of Bactrian camels arrived in town yesterday with a load of goods from the west. A large crowd soon gathered around the ugly beasts and curiously followed them to their place of unloading cargo. They carry immense loads and are hideous enough to frighten the natives out of the country.

The presence of these beasts in central Nevada was due to the fact that, in the mid-1850's, the War Department had experimented with them as a means of carrying supplies to its widely scattered military outposts throughout the arid southwest. However, the animals, while capable of bearing heavy burdens, failed to prove their worth — largely, it is said, because the rocky terrain over much of the area injured their feet — and the project was presently written off as a failure. Consequently, in 1863, the army authorities in Washington, who were then occupied with the more important matter of putting down the Rebellion, ordered that the camels be sold at auction.

Ownership of the herd thus passed into private hands, and in due time a group of a dozen or more were purchased by an Austin mill-owner and put to work carrying bags of salt from Walker Lake, close to the California border, over the more than a hundred miles of mountain and desert to the new town. Later, they were also used to transport other urgently needed supplies: provisions, merchandise, even parts of heavy mining machinery.

A month after the arrival of the first camel train in Austin, the paper published this dispatch from a correspondent in Star City, a long-since-vanished camp a few miles from Winnemucca:

THOSE CAMELS. — The camels got in at last — ten of them — carrying packs of nearly 600 pounds apiece. They were attended by a native Arabian from the south of Ireland. With his clay pipe in his mouth, and his red hair, he presented a very Oriental — and ornamental — appearance.

Two days later, on September 28, appeared this notice of the arrival of a second camel caravan at Austin:

Yesterday our citizens were again visited by the "ships of the desert," loaded with castings for one of our quartz mills. Four of them were bearers of burden, and four more, in the infantile class, were too young to be put under the pack. One could almost imagine himself in the East, among the hills of Judea, climbing the Lybian mountains, when he looked upon these patient animals, with their long, awkward gait, striding through the streets.

But despite their endurance, and the heavy loads they could carry, their use was presently abandoned and

groups of the picturesque animals were no longer encountered wending their way across Nevada's sage-
covered plains. Some were sold to owners of traveling
animal shows; others found refuge in zoos then being established in west coast cities. A number of them, however, were merely turned loose in the desert where, for a
generation or more, wayfarers in remote parts of the country were sometimes startled to come upon the ungainly
beasts. Reports of such encounters, indeed, have continued to crop up at intervals ever since, although the last
authenticated instance of their having been sighted was
many years ago, and it is assumed that the last remnants
of the herd have long since become extinct.

CHAPTER SEVEN

"Mule's Relief"

I

FROM the time the Reese River rush got under way and the first tents were pitched in Pony Canyon, few of the newcomers seem to have had any doubt at all on one point: that the town they were founding was there to stay. This, they were convinced, was to be no ninety-day wonder as had been a score of other Nevada camps since the discovery of the rich Comstock ledges three years earlier, no boom-or-bust hamlet into which the displaced coyotes would slink back before the next snows fell.

All through the chaotic first months, it was a rare resident, whether the newest of the johnny-come-latelies or a seasoned veteran of several weeks' standing, who did not firmly hold the view that he was in on an enterprise that was destined to make mining history. Consequently, the citizens looked impatiently ahead to the time when Austin would assume its place among the leading towns of the Territory. For, they argued, not only was it the center of the prodigiously rich Reese River mines, but also the natural supply and distribution point for all central Nevada. And that area, it was firmly believed, was destined to attract, not alone miners but numerous others, for none doubted that its fertile valleys needed only irrigation in order to raise bumper crops and support vast herds of cattle and sheep.

From the day of its first issue, the *Reveille* shared this bright view of Austin's future. Even after the unusually severe winter of 1863-1864 had stopped work on the mines and mills and brought the early boom to a temporary halt, the editor's faith was unshaken, and he missed no opportunity to refute articles appearing in the journals of rival mining towns hinting that the Reese River bubble had already burst. Thus, on March 5, 1864, appeared this answer to one such charge:

"Has anybody heard anything from Reese River lately? It was a great place four or five months ago, but like most earthly things its fame was evanescent. We have not heard of any bullion or any fortunes coming from there, though we have heard of 'dead broke' men who hailed from there. The newest humbug is always the greatest."

We clip the foregoing from the *Sierra Democrat* [a paper published in one of the California mother lode towns] of the 24th ult. For the benefit of the benighted individual from whose perceptive noodle it sprang, we will iterate the following, to most people, well-known facts. Austin today is more prosperous than any town in the Sierra in its most palmy days; its mines are not "evanescent" placers upon which Sierra built its "fame," but as lasting as the hills, and as Sierra dwindles will Austin rise to greatness. Our population is daily augmented by the arrival from all parts of California of those who would exchange the worn-out placers of that state for the more permanent, the everlasting, mines of this Territory. Scarcely a day passes that we do not ship bullion; a dozen mills are already in operation in town, and everything glides along most prosperously. Humbug! Come over here, Rip Van Winkle, and examine for yourself!

Some weeks later, on May 26, appeared this further reassurance to doubters of the town's permanence — including this time some local residents of little faith:

OUR FUTURE. — We, of the Reese River country, know whereof we speak when we predict that a good time is coming, and is not very distant, when we can show to outside barbarians, and the rest of mankind, that not only can we turn out the largest and purest bricks of silver, but that we have other sources of prosperity which, aside from our mineral deposits, will enable us to support a large population. At present we are a little feverish, visions of silver haunt the most unimaginative of us. We have made up our minds that, rich as the country is, it is not the country to spend one's days in. This feeling unfits us, to a very great extent, for that continuous exertion which is almost invariably the forerunner to success. Disappointment, which sooner or later ovetakes us all in our journey through life, will temper this inordinate longing for the fickle dame, and we shall make up our minds to live for the sake of living, rather than the almighty dollar. This good time is coming soon, and will be ushered in by the advent of schoolhouses (and school-marms, of course), and by the coming of the iron horse, when we can, inside of a fortnight, pay the "old folks at home" a visit, and be back again among our pretty girls and silver ledges.

The reference above to the iron horse is significant, for when they set out to enumerate the future blessings of their towns, few western editors of the period failed to list the coming of the railroad among the chief of these. For through the 1850's and early 1860's, residents all over the Pacific Coast were convinced that the region's isolation from the rest of the country was the greatest single factor retarding its development. With means of transportation between the two coasts limited to the slow, horse-drawn stages and freight wagons of the overland routes on the one hand and, on the other, the weeks-long voyages of steamers and sailing ships via Nicaragua, Panama, or round the Horn, all felt that this was a grievous disadvantage, both in their business and in their personal lives, and looked forward with impatience to the day when the much-debated transcontinental railroad would become a reality.

This feeling was particularly strong in Austin, and for good reason. For the Reese River country was one of the most isolated in the entire west. More than four hundred miles of mountains and desert separated it from San Francisco, its nearest shipping point, and with the cost of transporting goods from the metropolis ranging as high as twenty cents a pound, merchandise on the shelves of the town's shops was almost prohibitively high. Moreover — and of even greater importance — certain rich but refractory ores that could not be worked locally had to be cast aside, for it would have been too costly to ship them to eastern mills for reduction.

Consequently, Austin residents from the beginning awaited with particular impatience the day when their town would be connected with the rest of the world by that panacea of all economic ills, a railroad. Nor did they doubt that their hopes would be realized without much

delay. As early as November 7, 1863, the *Reveille* jubi-
lantly reprinted an editorial from the San Francisco *Call*
advocating that a local line then building in the Sacramento Valley be extended on eastward as far as the
Reese River and thus corner the lucrative business of its
rich new mines.

Putting itself solidly behind the project, the *Reveille*
stated that the road, which in its opinion could not fail to
return handsome profits to its owners, would require no
more than a year to build, and went on to list a number
of points that would make for economy of operation.
Among these, it pointed out the fact that, because the last
one hundred eighty miles of the route would pass
through arid, semidesert country, that part of the line
would be happily free of the inconvenience and danger
resulting from "having trees fall on the track."

When this project failed to materialize, Austin and the
Reveille looked hopefully toward another company recently organized in California. This was the Central Pacific which, under the guidance of a brilliant young engineer named Theodore D. Judah, had not only secured
the limited backing of a group of Sacramento merchants
but, more important, presently persuaded Congress to
grant subsidies liberal enough to assure its construction
eastward until its rails joined those of the Union Pacific
which was meanwhile preparing to build westward across
the plains toward the Rockies.

With the long-projected transcontinental line at last
assured, and with construction presently under way at
both ends, Austin breathed a sigh of relief, certain that
its isolation was soon to be a thing of the past. For, of
course, no one there doubted that the iron rails would

follow the well-traveled route of the overland stages and so pass through the town. Firm in that belief, residents looked confidently ahead to the time when Austin would assume its allotted place among the major cities of the west. Thus, on January 11, 1865, the *Reveille* announced triumphantly:

When the great Pacific Railroad is built, with its numerous branches leading to the neighboring rich mining districts, and Austin has become a large city, as it certainly will, then there will be no place as fit as this for the State Capitol. . . .

Soon, however, highly disturbing rumors began to circulate through the town. One was that the Central Pacific's surveying crews, engaged in laying preliminary lines across Nevada, were not following the overland trail but had swung far to the north and were driving their stakes along the banks of the Humboldt River. On learning that this was indeed the case, and that the projected road, if built as planned, would pass some ninety miles to the north of the town, the *Reveille* again shifted ground, abandoning its support of the faithless Central Pacific and coming out strongly in favor of yet another California railroad corporation.

Its new favorite was a recently organized enterprise called the San Francisco & Washoe, the announced objective of which was to corner the trade of the Comstock and other Nevada mining districts, including, of course, the booming Reese River. But in this hope, too, the paper and the town were speedily disillusioned. The San Francisco & Washoe never got beyond the planning stage, and Austin presently realized the bitter fact that it had been by-passed, that its nearest railroad connection would be at the village of Battle Mountain, ninety-two miles distant over a sandy, rutted road.

II

THE completion of the Central Pacific in 1869 of course brought to an end the brisk overland traffic that had flowed through the town since its founding. The daily arrival of the through stages, some heading east others west, which had long lent animation to the main street became a thing of the past. So likewise did the strings of dusty freight wagons and the numerous parties of immigrants rumbling westward in their traditional covered wagons. Austin, without quite realizing it, abruptly found itself at the end of an era, no longer on the main stream of east-west traffic but far removed from it, its isolation more complete than ever.

The consequence was that the townspeople grew more determined than before to get a railroad connection with the outer world. By then it had become not only an economic necessity but a matter of pride to its citizens. Moreover, although numerous delays and disappointments still lay ahead, their efforts were eventually crowned with success.

In 1874, five years after the completion of the Central Pacific, the *Reveille*, which had been regularly reporting the imminent formation of one or another company to build the road, none of which ever materialized, began publicizing the plans of still another group. The chief backer of this project, which from the first appeared to be more soundly financed than its predecessors, was one Michael J. Farrell, an official of the Manhattan Silver Mining Company which operated some of the most valuable mines and mills of the area.

Farrell's intention was to build a narrow-gauge road northward, following the course of the Reese River, to Battle Mountain, where it would connect with the Central Pacific. With the *Reveille* lending enthusiastic support both in its news columns and on the editorial page, the organization and preliminary planning went forward rapidly. At a special election, the voters of Lander County not only approved a bill giving the company a franchise to operate within its borders but granted its owners a subsidy of two hundred thousand dollars provided the line was completed and in operation within five years.

Thus far, all had gone well, but there were still difficult times ahead for the promoter and his associates. Before they could legally go into effect, both franchise and subsidy had to be approved by the state legislature, and by 1875 the practice of counties and other political subdivisions of going heavily into debt to finance railroads had come to be regarded with deep and usually well-founded suspicion. The result was that strong opposition to the measures was encountered among the legislators at Carson City, and Farrell — who had meantime had himself elected state senator from the Lander district — had a prolonged fight on his hands before getting his bills through both houses. Then, with that feat accomplished, came another setback. For Governor Bradley promptly vetoed the subsidy measure, thereby bringing down on his head the maledictions of the *Reveille,* which daily held him up to ridicule, terming him, among other things, "Old Broadhorns" and "His Ox-cellency," these being references to the governor's ownership of an extensive cattle ranch in the Washoe Valley. Whether because of the amusement these epithets aroused among the lawmakers, or for more sound reasons, Farrell was able to marshal sufficient strength to override the veto and the measure duly became law.

The promoter was then free to devote his energies to what proved to be the most difficult task of all: that of financing the building of the road, for the two hundred thousand dollars subsidy would, of course, not become available until the line was in operation. However, since Farrell had had the foresight to specify that the county subsidy would not expire for five years — surely ample time to build a ninety-mile road — no one was greatly concerned when his first attempts to induce eastern capitalists to invest in the project all ended in failure. The tireless promoter thereupon concluded that what was needed was more detailed and specific data on the cost of constructing and equipping the line, and — even more important — estimates of the heavy traffic that would flow over it once it was completed.

Accordingly, he prepared a series of rose-tinted reports emphasizing that the terrain over which it would pass presented no engineering difficulties, being over nearly all the entire distance as level as a floor, and forecasting the prodigious profits it would return to the lucky investors from its steadily growing volume of business. This last was to come, he maintained, not only from vastly increased mining activity in and about Austin, where the owners of numerous rich ledges were said to be awaiting only the cheaper freight rates the railroad would provide before going into full production, but from a number of promising new camps then springing up to the south and southeast. And of course he did not neglect to envision the substantial business the road would presently enjoy hauling the products of the farming communities soon to be founded in the Reese River and Big Smoky Valleys, plus large shipments of cattle and sheep from huge stock ranches that would one day occupy the foothill ranges for many miles about.

Not only did these sanguine forecasts appear in Farrell's reports; they were regularly echoed in the columns of the *Reveille*. Moreover, the industrious promoter repeated them in a steady stream of letters to investors on both coasts. Nor was it long before this double-barreled campaign began to get results — of a sort. The interest of first one group and then another was engaged to the point where representatives were sent out to make a first-hand survey of the road and its prospects. These were met at Battle Mountain by Farrell, conducted southward over the route of the proposed line to Austin where they were greeted by a committee of prominent citizens, taken on tours of the mines and mills, tendered a banquet, and accorded all the attentions due honored guests.

Despite this lavish hospitality, however, the reports the agents rendered to their principals seem to have been uniformly unfavorable, for in each case the ultimate answer was No. Thus more than three of the allotted five years passed and Austin's chance for a railroad appeared to be as remote as ever. Meantime, the new town of Eureka, some seventy miles farther east — which had not even been in existence when Austin began its campaign for a railroad — had entered the race; what is more, it promptly found the backing for which the other town was still futilely seeking. With funds put up by the Bank of California in San Francisco, then the dominant financial house of the entire coast, the Eureka & Palisade Railroad was built in record time and by 1876 was operating trains connecting with the Central Pacific at Palisade, some eighty-five miles to the north.

Understandably, this development had a depressing effect on Austin, whose citizens by then had come to believe that their hopes for a railroad, once so bright, were unlikely ever to be realized. Even the *Reveille's* editor, whose faith and support had remained strong through many earlier disappointments, now began to waver, and he presently began referring to the long-deferred road as "Farrell's Folly."

Events were to prove, however, that this dark hour was but the prelude to a far brighter dawn. For early in 1878 promoter Farrell succeeded in engaging the interest of a Colonel Lyman Briggs, one of the most eminent railroad engineers of the country. Briggs came west, went over the route with Farrell, and listened while Austin's mine-owners and businessmen went through their routine of entertaining the guest and forecasting the heavy traffic the road would enjoy.

At the end of his stay, the visitor electrified the town by announcing that he considered the plan sound from every standpoint. Moreover, he stated that he had so reported to the eastern financiers who had sent him out and who in the past had made numerous similar investments upon his recommendation. The consequence was that a week or two later, a party of New York capitalists arrived on the scene and, having checked and approved Briggs's findings, proceeded to incorporate the Nevada Railroad and to name Briggs chief engineer.

Thereafter, events moved rapidly. Surveys got promptly under way and were completed in May 1878, and the *Reveille*, its recent doubts forgotten, announced triumphantly that Austin would hear the long-awaited blasts of a locomotive's whistle before the end of that year. On July 4, the town's traditional parade had in the place of honor an elaborate float forecasting the coming event: a replica of a train, complete with Palace cars, smoke issuing from the funnel of its locomotive, and with the tender proudly bearing the legend, Nevada Railroad.

III

ENTHUSIASM remained high throughout the summer. When, however, first weeks and then months passed and the construction crews that were daily expected unaccountably failed to show up, the hopes of the townspeople again waned. Presently, Colonel Briggs announced that stock in the company was proving difficult to sell and that building necessarily would have to be delayed until the financing was completed. Meantime, the year 1878 ended, and only twelve months remained before the two hundred thousand dollars subsidy would expire. The prospects, already dark enough, became measurably more so when, a few weeks later, word reached Austin that the

Nevada Railroad's backers, having failed to raise the necessary capital, had given up the ghost and retired from the field.

Then, toward the end of August — and only five months before the subsidy deadline — the town learned that a well-known New York financial firm, the Phelps-Stokes Corporation, which had large holdings of mines and mills in the Austin area, had taken over the project and planned to push it through with all speed. Moreover, it soon grew clear that the new company, which called itself the Nevada Central, meant business. A contract to build the line was promptly awarded to General James Ledlie, a Civil War veteran who had supervised much of the construction of the eastern half of the transcontinental road, and, on September 1, the first shovelful of earth was ceremoniously turned at Battle Mountain.

With, after more than four years and a half of delay, the building of the road actually under way, Austin's enthusiasm again mounted. Through the weeks that followed, the *Reveille's* daily accounts of progress were read with keen interest — an interest that was sharpened by the knowledge that the rail-laying was now literally a race against time.

Suspense over the outcome built up steadily during the remaining months of 1879, with each day bringing the deadline — February 9, 1880 — closer. General Ledlie, putting additional crews in the field as fast as men and equipment could be assembled, had the first twenty miles graded by the end of September. By mid-October, track had been laid for half a dozen miles out of Battle Mountain and workmen at nine different camps were preparing the roadbed over the remaining eighty miles to

Austin. Meantime, rolling stock was being purchased from other railroads all over the west, there being no time to have it built, and besides, the owners were economy-minded. Colonel Briggs, who had been retained as chief engineer, visited narrow-gauge lines in California and elsewhere, picking up an engine here, a few flatcars there, and passenger coaches — even rails, turntables, switches, and other equipment — wherever available.

By Thanksgiving, track had been laid more than a third of the way from Battle Mountain and the road began to pick up a bit of business, with a daily train carrying passengers and freight to the railhead where they were transferred to stages or wagons for the remainder of the journey to Austin.

By then, however, the builders had a new cause for worry, for the time was approaching when winter, always severe on the high plateaus of central Nevada, would close in, freezing the ground and making grading and track-laying doubly difficult. As if this were not enough, the gangs of tough construction workers chose that time to go on strike, demanding an improvement in the quality and quantity of the food served them in company mess-wagons, as well as an increase in wages, then a munificent $1.25 per day. Contractor Ledlie met this crisis by importing strike-breakers and by rounding up the ringleaders and shipping them back to Battle Mountain with a warning to keep moving. The remaining strikers thereupon returned to work and the race continued.

From then on the tension heightened as the struggle neared its climax. Throughout December, with wintry blasts and freezing temperatures adding to the problems, the work went on at a steadily increasing tempo. By then the construction force numbered close to six hundred, many of them employees of Austin mines and mills that had shut down for the winter. This augmented army, working now in two ten-hour shifts, swarmed over the uncompleted section, laboriously smoothing the frozen roadbed to receive the ties and rails, and the railhead advanced southward at an average rate of two miles a day. Despite these herculean efforts, however, by Christmas day — with a scant six weeks remaining — the long-awaited sound of a locomotive's whistle still could not be heard in Austin. The end of track was more then twenty miles distant and by then the ground was so solidly frozen that scrapers could no longer be used and all grading had to be done with pick and shovel.

Nonetheless, General Ledlie, although he must have had his moments of doubt, remained the picture of confidence as he periodically issued reassuring statements to the public, which the *Reveille* obligingly published. On the last day of the year, the first annual meeting of the Nevada Central stockholders was held at Battle Mountain. Following a bountiful dinner, at which Lander County officials were honored guests, the General and Chief Engineer Briggs expressed confidence that the trains would be running into Austin well before the final day. But as luck would have it, the winter proved a particularly severe one, with storm succeeding storm throughout January and the work falling so far behind schedule that on February 5, with only four days remaining, the nearest track was still some ten miles up the valley.

At that point, however, the weather belatedly proved

co-operative and in bright sunshine all hands put forth a final effort. So fast was progress that by February 8 the remaining distance had been cut in half and, the day being Sunday, great crowds came out from Austin to view the spectacle and cheer the workmen on.

Construction continued throughout the night and when the final day — Monday the ninth — dawned, three miles remained to go. By midday this had been reduced to two miles, but then came a new misfortune. A work-train bearing the rails needed to bring the tracks to the city limits was stalled somewhere up the line, and word came that it could not possibly arrive before the time limit expired at midnight.

With what seemed certain failure staring them in the face, the Nevada Central's officials thought fast, for they, along with everyone else in Austin, recognized that only a near-miracle could stave off defeat. Fortunately, the men in charge, together with the town's leaders, proved equal to the emergency. Following a conference late in the afternoon, members of the town council were summoned to a special meeting at the city hall. There the mayor addressed them, pointing out that General Ledlie's forces, who by then had laid tracks to within a mile of the city limits, had on hand enough rails to proceed only another eight hundred yards. Thus, he continued, the company, whose railroad would mean so much to Austin's future, stood to lose the Lander County subsidy by the narrowest of margins, a disaster that would throw the line into bankruptcy at the very moment it was ready to begin operation. Moreover, went on the mayor, they were all aware of the manifold benefits the railroad would bring the town. Because of it, Austin's future was assured; with mines and mills going into full production and with all phases of business booming, a large increase in population could confidently be expected. Why not prepare now for that influx by providing more space for new industries and for sites on which the newcomers could build their homes? What he was proposing, he concluded, was a moderate extension of the city's limits; specifically, that its boundaries be moved northward for a distance of half a mile.

The councilmen saw the point; the ordinance was hastily drawn up and unanimously passed. Word of this action reached the railhead just as darkness was falling, and while a final half-mile of track remained to be laid before the new city boundary would be reached. Hundreds of townspeople gathered along the right of way, building bonfires to ward off the subzero cold and cheering the workers as they strove valiantly to close the gap. In the best tradition of wild west melodrama, the outcome remained in doubt to the very end. Then, with the minute hand of scores of watches in the hands of onlookers creeping inexorably up toward midnight, a final pair of rails were hurried into place and loosely spiked down, and in stentorian tones General Ledlie announced that the Nevada Central had entered Austin.

The celebration that followed was one of the most tempestuous in the annals of the town. Brief ceremonies, including the driving of three spikes of Austin silver, were held at the end of track, following which the chilled but hilarious throng hurried up the canyon to the middle of the town where for the rest of the night round after round of toasts to the success of the road were drunk in Main Street's score of bars.

IV

AS EVENTS were to prove, the little railroad had from its beginning urgent need for the support, and patronage, of its well-wishers. For the hard fact of the matter was that by the time Austin got its long-deferred railroad its period of prosperity had already passed. By 1880, the rich ledges on which its fame had rested had all pinched out and the discovery of other deposits of millable ore was growing less frequent year by year. Moreover, the new mining districts to the south and southeast, of which Austin had expected so much, had failed to live up to their promise and one by one the camps were being abandoned as the miners hurried off to yet newer fields. Finally, the farming and stock-raising industries which, according to the *Reveille,* were soon to transform the Reese River Valley into a veritable garden spot, remained as far from realization as ever.

All of this of course meant far less business for the Nevada Central than its builders had envisioned. In the beginning, the road operated three daily trains each way; after only a few weeks, however, the small volume of traffic caused two of these to be withdrawn. Thereafter, one combination freight and passenger train left Battle Mountain each morning, made the ninety miles to Austin in seven and a half hours, and returned to its starting place that night.

With this drastic cut in service, plus rigid economies in operation and maintenance, the road during the first several years managed to keep out of the red and even to pay an occasional modest dividend. Meantime, there had been a number of changes of ownership, the first of which was its sale by the Phelps-Stokes interests to the Union Pacific, owner of the eastern half of the transcontinental road. When news reached Austin that the powerful Union Pacific had taken over the road, many of the townspeople, including the *Reveille's* editor, were convinced that the parent company intended to extend it on southward to connect with a line it was planning to build from Salt Lake to southern California. For a few months, Austin believed that it was soon to have direct connections with two large railroad systems, with the resulting competition bringing about a sharp reduction of freight and passenger rates.

Although this project, like a number of other proposed extensions of the Nevada Central, never materialized, one short feeder line was actually built, and in that Austin took a particular pride. As railroads went, this was no very impressive venture, being only a little more than a mile in length, but it gave the town a distinction enjoyed by no other city in the state, namely, a street-car system. For the Nevada Central's original terminus was on the site of the former town of Clifton, at a point on the valley floor opposite the mouth of Pony Canyon. It was in order to avoid the expense and inconvenience of transporting passengers and freight from the station up the steep grade to the center of the town that the Austin City Railroad was planned and built during the summer of 1880. This was a narrow-gauge line that wound up the canyonside and continued the length of Main Street, its motive power being supplied by teams of sturdy mules.

For a few months, the little mule-drawn trains of Austin's City Railroad were a familiar sight as they were laboriously pulled up from below and, on their return trips, propelled then by gravity, coasted back to their starting point at a far livelier clip. In mid-November, however, one of the Nevada Central's locomotives ventured onto the City Railroad's tracks and, puffing mightily, managed to make the ascent. Accordingly, a steam dummy was ordered from an eastern manufacturer and, with the name "Mule's Relief" painted on its sides, presently took over the task. Later the name of its Austin extension came to be applied to the entire road, which became known to several generations of Nevadans as the "Mule's Relief."

The subsequent history of the Nevada Central was one long struggle against adversity. The Reese River mines, which were expected to enter a new and more active era with the coming of the railroad, failed to make the looked-for revival; instead, the leading producers one by one closed down until, by the mid-1890's, not a single major company remained in operation. With the collapse of its chief — and indeed almost its only — industry, many of the residents left and the town's population, which had once numbered from six to eight thousand, rapidly declined until by the end of the century less than a tenth that number remained.

Visitors during the early 1900's found the place already taking on the aspect of a ghost town, with scores of houses and cabins perched on the canyonsides standing vacant and forlorn and with the iron shutters permanently closed on more than half the business structures on the main street. As late as 1910, one visitor's curiosity was aroused by the fact that on peering through the windows of several stores he could see their stocks still intact within, with showcases and other fixtures undisturbed and piles of merchandise collecting dust on the shelves. He was told that during a depression of the early 1890's the owners of such establishments had simply locked the doors and left, their stocks not being worth what it would have cost to transport them elsewhere.

Yet throughout these years, the little railroad somehow managed to keep functioning, although the number of its trains had, by 1905, dropped from one a day to three a week. Often these carried no freight at all, the "train" consisting only of a single car powered by a gasoline motor and bearing nothing more than a few bags of mail and an occasional passenger. Presently the struggling line was called to face a potent new threat: the rise of the automobile and the competition of motor trucks. This marked the beginning of the end, although, operating now with equipment hopelessly antiquated and with its roadbed in deplorable condition, it continued for several decades longer.

Not until 1937 did the little Central Nevada, with which Austin's fortunes had for so long been bound up, cease to run, and the moldering town found itself once more, as it had been more than half a century earlier, without railroad connection with the outer world.

CHAPTER EIGHT

The Sagebrush Linnet

I

DURING Civil War days, the exploits of grocer Gridley and his sack of flour made him by far the most widely known personage the little mining town had produced. That distinction he maintained unchallenged for well over a decade. As the 1880's opèned, however, a formidable rival appeared on the scene in the person of a slight, dark-haired young woman who had spent her childhood romping on Austin's slanting streets.

The first mention of this future notable in the columns of the *Reveille* was toward the end of 1870. At services held on Christmas Eve at an Austin church, one feature of the entertainment, a hymn sung by two local residents, was particularly pleasing to those present. The pair must have presented an odd spectacle, for while one — who was known as the Baron von Netzer — was a man of mature years and a vocalist of local renown, his companion was a ten-year-old girl and this was her first public appearance. Nonetheless, their duet seems to have made a lasting impression, for on December 27 the paper printed a long and admiring letter from a music-lover who signed himself "Orpheus." This is the concluding paragraph:

With the fine voice of the Baron, church-goers are sufficiently familiar; it remains, therefore, only to say a few words of praise in respect to the part sung by Miss Wixom. Considering the extreme youthfulness of the gifted cantatrice, and the few opportunities afforded to train her voice, it was really a rich treat to listen to her almost pure soprano, executed with an ease and finish truly astonishing in one so young, and not often met with outside professional circles. After having listened to the performance . . . I fully coincide with the view expressed by you in these columns of the entire practicability of establishing a Choral Society in Austin. . . .

An Austin Choral Society duly came into existence a few months later, but whether as a result of this letter, or the singing of young Miss Wixom, does not appear. More important, however, is the fact that this marked the entry into the public prints of an artist who was presently to win international renown and bring Austin a degree of fame second only to that of her silver mines.

For from the 1880's onward, the career of "Emmy" Wixom was by all odds the town's favorite success story, and it remains so to this day. Born in the tiny mining town of Alpine in the northern California foothills, she was taken to Austin some four years later by her physician father. There she passed the next nine years, one of the group of children who attended the local school, explored Pony Canyon during the summer vacations and in winter coasted down its steep inclines. During all that time, it is said that singing was her chief pleasure and, following her first public appearance in 1870, she was in so much demand at church sociables and other prim

gatherings that by the time she reached her teens her untutored but singularly melodious voice had made her a
prime favorite in the town.

Then, in 1873, her mother having died, Dr. Wixom
took her down to California and enrolled her as a board-
ing student at Mills Seminary at Fruitvale, across the bay
from San Francisco. Mills was then the Coast's most eminent and fashionable school for girls, to which the daughters of prosperous citizens not only in California but in
Virginia City and other Nevada boom towns were almost
invariably sent. There the Austin girl, who became
known to her classmates as "Wixie," became a pupil of
the seminary's German vocal teacher, Alfred Kelleher,
who for the next three years put her through a rigorous
course of training, and to whom she later gave credit
for having laid the groundwork of her musical education.

As had been the case at Austin, the girl's voice, by then
a clear soprano of unusual quality and range, promptly
attracted attention in her new environment, and she not
only appeared regularly in the seminary's weekly musi-
cals but was often called on by Principal Susan Mills to
entertain groups of visitors. It was, indeed, mainly due to
Mrs. Mills's patronage that, following the girl's gradua-
tion in 1876, she was able to carry out what by then had
become her major ambition: that of continuing her musical education in Europe. For by the mid-1870's Austin's
brief period of prosperity had already waned, and Dr.
Wixom — who, like most of the solvent citizens of the
town, had invested heavily in its mines — found himself
unable to finance his daughter's studies abroad. Mrs.
Mills accordingly arranged to have the girl travel with

the naturalist Dr. Adrian Ebell, and his wife, who were leaving for a protracted sojourn in Paris. Soon after their arrival, however, Dr. Ebell died, and when the widow accompanied his body home the girl was left alone with, according to one friend, "far more ambition than money."

It was not long, however, before she found a new benefactress, this one in the person of the formidable Marie Hungerford Mackay, wife of John W. Mackay, the immensely wealthy Comstock silver king. In many respects, the lives of Mrs. Mackay and her young protégée had run in parallel channels. Both had lived in the camps of the California mother lode and in the raw silver towns of Nevada before taking up residence in Paris, and both had been led to take the latter step because of a deep and all-consuming ambition, one to become an opera star, the other a social leader.

Moreover, by the time of Miss Wixom's arrival in Paris, Mrs. Mackay, backed by her husband's bottomless purse, plus good looks, an amiable disposition, and a considerable native shrewdness, had already made notable strides toward achieving her goal. By establishing herself in an impressive mansion on the rue Tilset, where she entertained in a truly regal style, and by giving generous support to currently fashionable French charities, she had by 1876 made herself a figure of consequence in the social life of the capital.

Just how important a part Mrs. Mackay had in launching her fellow Nevadan on her operatic career has long been a matter of debate. While some have given her the major credit, others who were close associates of the girl after her rise to stardom, including her manager-husband, Dr. Raymond Palmer, stated that the wealthy American woman gave her but little aid, financial or in other ways. In any event, the girl was presently accepted as a pupil by Madame Mathilde Marchesi, one of the foremost vocal teachers of the day, who, in the course of her long career trained such stars as Gerster, Melba, di Murska, Eames, and Calvé. After a year in Paris, the girl continued on to Vienna, then the musical capital of Europe, and, having by then definitely determined on an operatic career, she adopted for professional use the name of the sagebrush state, becoming Emma Nevada.

Meantime, her father continued to practice in Austin and from time to time the *Reveille* printed bits of news concerning her. Thus, on August 24, 1878, appeared this brief item:

ALPINE FLOWERS. — Dr. Wixom received by mail this morning from Vienna, Austria, some wild flowers gathered on the slopes of the Alps by his daughter Emma. The flowers are pressed and arranged on a card in the form of a wreath. The Doctor reports that Miss Emma is making excellent progress in her musical education.

Something more than two years later, on January 3, 1881, this longer story told the ever-interested townspeople that the local girl was then well launched on her professional career:

EMMA NEVADA. — A gentleman in this city from Newark, N. J., favored us with a batch of late Eastern newspapers, among which were copies of the *Newark Daily Advertiser.* In one of the latter appears a correspondence to that paper from Trieste, Austria, of date Nov. 20, 1880, from which we make an extract as follows, complimentary to our Miss Emma Wixom, or Emma Nevada:

Just now the musical public of Trieste is quite wild with excitement over the singing of a young American lady whose professional name is Emma Nevada, from the state to which she belongs. Her real name is Emma Wixom, the daughter of W. W. Wixom, an eminent physician and surgeon of Austin, Nev. She is not quite twenty years of age. Three years ago last June she graduated at Mills Seminary at Oakland, Cal., a brilliant scholar, and with the reputation for being a musical prodigy. That same summer she was sent to Europe and placed at Vienna under the training of the best drill-masters now in Europe.

Her proficiency in the acquisition of musical culture, and the development of a voice of very rare excellence, was a source of amazement even to her teachers. During the two and a half years she was in Vienna, such was the purity and force of her character that during the entire time she took her place as organist and singer in the little English Protestant Church — Dissenter — whose pastor was repeatedly arrested by the police as an over-zealous Protestant propagandist. In this way the young lady, with all her devotion to music, failed to hear "the Philharmonicia," so famous in Vienna, which is rendered only on Sunday!

This young lady has received the highest commendations from the Musical Director of Italy and other musical authorities, and is to sing in the Scala at Milan the coming Winter and Spring. Seven nights she has sung in

Trieste to overrunning houses, and although I have not yet heard her, my musical friend, Mr. Consul Thayer, says she is a prodigy whose compass, power and wonderful richness of voice exceed anything he had ever heard.

Her engagements at Trieste in the fall of 1880 were not the young singer's first professional appearance, for she had made her debut at London earlier that year in the opera *La Sonnambula*. Thereafter, the *Reveille* was at pains to keep its readers informed on the rocketlike rise of what it proudly termed "our Emma," frequently reprinting excerpts from eastern papers reporting the successive triumphs of the new American star in various European cities.

Then, early in 1884, came the news for which the entire town — and, indeed, music-lovers all over the nation — had been impatiently waiting: that the American impresario, Colonel James Henry Mapleson, had added the new sensation to his star-studded troupe, and that during the coming season Nevada would be heard in the leading cities of the country, including those on the west coast.

II

GREAT was the public's anticipation when, traveling in four luxuriously appointed "parlor cars," the company, which included not only Nevada but the incomparable Adelina Patti, reached San Francisco in mid-March of 1885. On the day tickets went on sale for Nevada's first appearance, block-long queues formed hours before the box-office opened and the entire house was promptly sold out, many of the choicest seats going to speculators. It was announced that she would open on the evening of March 18, as Amina in *La Sonnambula,* a part in which she had several weeks earlier scored an ovation at the Academy of Music in New York.

However, word presently got about that the lady was unwell, and as the opening date drew near, anxious ticket-holders plied both Mapleson and her manager with questions about her condition. Dr. Palmer, who was her physician as well as her manager — and who before the year was out would become her husband, too — announced that her first appearance would definitely have to be postponed. She had, he stated, had neuralgia at New Orleans, two teeth had been pulled at Salt Lake City — in proof of which he produced the teeth from his pocket and exhibited them to the interested reporters — moreover, she had been confined to her bed with tonsillitis during the balance of the trip west, and since her arrival had left her Palace Hotel suite only for one brief afternoon ride in Golden Gate Park.

Colonel Mapleson, on the other hand, was just as positive that she would be in excellent voice on the appointed night. He had, he confided to the press, "been looking down singers' throats for thirty years," and the public could take his word for it that as far as Nevada was concerned there was nothing to be uneasy about. Opera singers, he added, were always worrying about the condition of their throats, it was a sort of occupational disease with them, but he had observed that when the time came, they could be depended on to make miraculous recoveries and give superb performances. Not for nothing did the *Alta California* term him "the Napoleon of Managers."

The canny Mapleson's reassuring words may have been due to the fact that the town's speculators, who stood to lose heavily if Nevada failed to sing on the eighteenth, were threatening to sue him should there be a last-minute change of program. Nonetheless, a day or two later, the rumored switch was duly made; on the morning of the seventeenth, the papers announced that another opera would be presented the following night and that *La Sonnambula* had been postponed until the twenty-third.

This delay, however, merely increased the ardor of the Californians, and of what one paper described as "the trainloads" of Nevadans who had journeyed to San Francisco to hear her. Columns-long stories in all the local journals the next day made it clear that the occasion was one long to be remembered; the *Examiner* stated that when the petite singer stepped to the footlights at the end of the first act, she received "the greatest ovation ever seen in this state," and another reported that "the enthusiasm bordered on lunacy."

"Nothing could have been more charming [wrote the *Alta's* critic] than when she bowed her acknowledgment to the shouts of 'Bravo' that were showered on her," and went on to describe how, in response to shouts for "Home, Sweet Home," from the audience, she was overcome by emotion and had to retire to the wings, then reappeared and, "with moistened eyes," sang the ballad. "A perfect furore was the result. Mlle Nevada . . . crowned Arditi [the conductor] with one of her laurel wreaths . . . then, with the grace of a child she gathered her floral offerings and tripped off the stage. . . ."

At the end of the second act, the demonstration reached still greater heights, with the diva obliging with more ballads, then calling Mapleson to the footlights to share the applause, while from orchestra and gallery masses of flowers rained down on the stage, and "bouquet after bouquet, intended for Nevada, grazed the manager's bald pate."

Conspicuous among the scores of floral tributes, all meticulously described, were a huge laurel wreath presented by one hundred twenty-six of her Mills Seminary classmates and bearing the legend: "With Fragrant Bloom, and Living Green, We Crown Thee Song's Victorious Queen," and, from Mrs. Mills, a basket enclosed in a satin case, on the top of which was "a branch of apple blossoms, on which was perched a linnet," the last being in recognition of the fact that the west had conferred on the singer the title of "the Sagebrush Linnet."

On the following Saturday afternoon, Nevada crossed the bay to Fruitvale and there renewed old school acquaintances, sang "The Last Rose of Summer" and "The Mocking Bird" and other favorite ballads to the assembled guests, and was presented with yet other tokens of esteem, among them, a silver vase, a satin glove case, a scarf pin, and "a purse of $2000 in five-dollar gold pieces, which was furnished by subscription through the efforts of former pupils at Mills. . . ."

Then, after appearing in two other operas, *Lucia di Lammermoor* and *Mireille,* and having for two weeks "been accorded the honors and adulation usually reserved for a reigning queen," she and the company headed east again, opening in Chicago on April 6, then on to New York, Boston, and Philadelphia before sailing to keep a London engagement beginning in June.

Before the year 1885 ended, however, she was again on the west coast, this time on a concert tour, her company, consisting of tenor, baritone, pianist, flutist, and director, traveling by private car. Curiously, on this second visit, she scored far less of a triumph. This was attributed to the fact that the others of the group, all Europeans, were "mediocre singers," the San Francisco *Chronicle* stating severely that "If Mme. Nevada had selected a company of clever American singers she would have done herself more credit." Besides, there were those who thought the price of seats, which ranged upward to four dollars, was excessive for a concert, even though her first appearance, on November 16, marked the opening of San Francisco's newest playhouse, the Alcazar, which one local scribe termed "incomparably the prettiest theatre in America."

Perhaps, too, there was another reason why San Franciscans this time were able to hold their enthusiasm well in check. Since her last visit, she had married her physician-manager, Raymond Palmer, and in so doing had in the public estimation lost some of what the *Alta* had called "the naivete and sweetness . . . which endears her to her audiences." There was indeed a touch of asperity in the review of the *Oakland Tribune's* critic who wrote that although Nevada had performed creditably, the other artists left much to be desired; of her husband he commented brusquely: "The Doctor is decidedly unpopular."

But if her four San Francisco concerts were a disappointment, the memory of them must have been obliterated by the warmth of her reception at her next two appearances. For, on leaving the coast, her car, the "Nevada," headed over the Sierra, with two stops scheduled in the Sagebrush State. The first was at Virginia City, which she reached on the morning of December 3, to find a crowd of some two thousand gathered about the station. She acknowledged their uproarious welcome while standing on the rear platform of a Virginia & Truckee day-coach — the "Nevada" being too big to pass through the tunnels of that corkscrew line — then entered a landau drawn by four black horses and, with her husband, her father, Dr. Wixom, and two members of her company, rode the length of C Street to the house of her Mills classmate, Mrs. W. E. Sharon, wife of the town's leading banker, where she was to stay during her brief visit.

On the following night, December 4, Piper's Opera House was crowded to the doors, some three hundred extra seats having been placed on the stage, in the aisles, and at other vantage points. This, her "first appearance before an audience in the state upon the name of which she has shed luster by her talents" was a duplication of her initial performance in San Francisco eight months earlier, with scores of elaborate floral pieces being passed over the footlights and the wildly applauding audience demanding, and receiving, encore after encore. It was in a radiant mood that she and her company hurried from the opera house to the station at eleven that night and set off for Austin, her second Nevada stop and her real homecoming.

Of the little silver town's welcome to its famous daughter, the San Francisco *Chronicle's* correspondent wrote on December 7:

Emma Nevada met with an enthusiastic and flattering reception on the occasion of her visit to the home of her youth in Austin last Friday evening. She was brought from Battle Mountain to Clifton on a special train over the Nevada Central, and driven to town in a four-in-hand carriage. As the vehicle bearing the queen of song entered the city, the Lander Guard Band struck up "Home, Sweet Home," and the enthusiastic populace un-hitched the horses from the carriage and drew her in triumph to the Molinelli House [a local hotel]. She gave a concert in the Methodist Church in the evening, and was the recipient of an ovation that will no doubt be treasured as a green spot in her memory to the day of her death. The building was crowded and at the end of her rendition of "Home, Sweet Home," the audience rose to its feet and cheered for a space of five minutes. The stage was loaded with floral offerings in which the fragrant sage of this state was mingled with the fairest flowers from California. . . .

This account of "Emmy" Wixom's welcome home was, however, a model of restraint as compared with that published in the *Reveille*, which paid homage to the local girl's return at such length, and with such a wealth of admiring detail, that upon her departure she must have carried away with her the comforting knowledge that not in years had the town witnessed an event so memorable.

Thereafter, the singer made her headquarters at places far removed from Austin. She lived in England, first at London and then, after her retirement to private life, at Wevertree, a suburb of Liverpool, where she died on June 4, 1940. In 1902, she had paid her last visit to the west coast, one of the highlights of which had been a pilgrimage to her birthplace in the little foothill village of Alpine in the California mother lode. There is no record, however, that she ever again set foot on the slanting streets of the Nevada town where as a child she had scored her first triumphs.

CHAPTER NINE

Don't Call It a Ghost Town

I

NOT only was Austin, even during its otherwise turbulent first years, largely free of outbreaks of violence and other forms of lawlessness; it also long escaped a type of disaster then frequent in all western mining towns, namely, a major fire. To be sure, there were occasional small blazes, usually the result of sparks from the town's hundreds of wood stoves, or from overturned kerosene lamps or lanterns. However, these were invariably extinguished before serious damage was done, a circumstance that the *Reveille* attributed to the efficiency of Austin's volunteer fire department. Perhaps, however, the chief reason why the town so long avoided severe losses from that source was the fact that, lumber being a scarce and expensive commodity in that treeless country, most of the buildings in the business section were constructed of such fire-resistant materials as the native rock and adobe bricks.

Commenting on the town's good fortune in this respect, the *Reveille* stated on August 27, 1878:

It is a remarkable fact that, during the fifteen years of existence of Austin as a town, an insurance company has never been called upon to pay one dollar of insurance on property destroyed by fire within the corporate limits.

Perhaps the property-owners, reassured by items of that sort, came to believe that their town was immune to such visitations and so frugally cut down on their insurance policies or else let them lapse entirely. In any event, when, on August 9, 1881, the long-delayed conflagration came, the fire's victims proved to be woefully underinsured, collecting only fifteen thousand dollars on a loss said to have exceeded one hundred thousand. The fire, starting in midmorning in a watchmaker's shop in the east side of Main Street, spread so rapidly that, reported the *Reveille*, "in less than five minutes, four or five frame buildings were enveloped." Although the town's firemen responded with their usual promptness and the reservoir atop the hill to the north contained ample water, for some reason pressure was low in the mains and the streams played on the blazing buildings were feeble and ineffectual.

A moderate summer wind blowing up the canyon caused the flames to advance steadily, consuming all in their path until, more than an hour later, their progress was halted at an intersecting street just below the courthouse. Next day the *Reveille*, the plant of which had narrowly escaped, listed the following structures destroyed: the Odd Fellows and Masonic Hall, the telegraph office, the Elred Block, the Post Office, Wright's Drug Store, Parrott & McGamb's blacksmith shop, a livery stable, photograph gallery, two barber shops, and five saloons. Several days later, the Virginia City *Chronicle*, calling to mind the *Reveille's* boast the town had never had a serious fire, commented: "We will say this for Austin: it doesn't often go in for that sort of thing but when it does it puts on an A-1 show."

It was, however, not fire but flood that constituted Austin's chief source of danger. Because its entire business area, including stores, hotels, and public buildings, fronted on a main street that followed the trough of the canyon for more than a mile, any unusually heavy rainstorm presented a problem, with water to a depth of several inches covering the thoroughfare from curb to curb and sometimes making it necessary for merchants to lay down little sandbag dykes to keep it from flowing into their doorways.

During the first fifteen years, these measures of coping with the problem had proved effectual; in consequence, the residents had come to look on the periodical visitations as an annoyance rather than a source of real danger. That, however, was before the summer of 1878. On the morning of August 13, towering black clouds gathered above the Toiyabe Range, rapidly assumed the proportions of a cloudburst and sent an unprecedented volume of water roaring down Pony Canyon into the town.

Four days later, on the seventeenth, the Sacramento *Union* printed this dispatch from Austin describing the disaster that had followed:

. . . In a few minutes the flood was a raging torrent, running a river from three to ten feet deep. Destruction marked every step of its path . . . The *Reveille* building, a one-story brick, was the first to go; then followed sidewalks, porches, awnings and merchandise, cattle, wagons, wood, timbers and fragments of small buildings. The sight was a frightful one to behold. . . . One man, named Sparum, was washed out of the Philadelphia Brewery, at the lower end of town, and later in the evening his body was found a mile below, stripped naked. . . .

The scene this morning [the fourteenth] is a sad one. The main street is completely gutted, and every house filled three or four feet deep with sand and debris. The *Reveille* is a complete ruin. One of the compositors had a narrow escape. When the building commenced to fill with water he climbed to some timbers supporting the roof, and when the crash came he was buried in the ruins but managed to break through a skylight.

An effort will be made by the *Reveille* proprietors to get out some sort of paper today. Their office is simply "gone up the flue," but they hope to fish a few type out of the wreck . . .

It was not, however, until August 19, six days after the disaster, that the little paper was able to resume publication. Its appearance gave striking evidence of the difficulties under which it had been produced: the paper on which it was printed was wrinkled and water-stained; the text — mainly a listing of the damage done to the stricken town — was set in several sizes of type, and its entire back page was blank save for the words "The Flood" printed in the center of each column.

The journal's reappearance so soon after the catastrophe was warmly welcomed by its contemporaries in California and Nevada, the Elko *Independent* commenting on August 29 on "the indomitable pluck of Booth and Hart . . . who, notwithstanding the appalling wreck and ruin of their office . . . literally dug out from the slime and boulders sufficient printing material to issue a half-sheet of that wide-awake journal on Monday last."

The *Reveille*, as was its custom, took misfortune in

its stride, enlivening its accounts of the desolation with occasional touches of wry humor. The editor had for years been conducting a campaign to beautify the town by planting trees on its main street and so providing welcome shade during the hot summers. Considerable progress had been made in carrying out that program; in its issue of August 23, however, he reported:

NO MORE TREES. — The last flood settled the question of trees on Main Street. The cloudburst of 1873 carried away several rows of flourishing locusts, and the last one ripped up all the trees but one on the Court House embankment, and the line of pretty maples in front of the International Hotel. It is not likely that another tree will ever be planted on Main Street.

Several weeks passed before the paper, having rehabilitated its plant, again assumed its normal appearance. Meanwhile, sidelights on the flood continued to appear from time to time. On August 27 came this brief item:

The Carson *Appeal* says it doesn't like to exhibit too much feeling, but the appearance of the *Reveille* is very "sedimental." It refers to the dried mud which adorns the edges of some of the papers we print. We can't help it; we have none but cloudbursted paper on hand, but as soon as paper now on the way from San Francisco arrives we will give the *Appeal* a clean sheet.

Two days later appeared an advertisement of a local resident, C. C. Bartlett, seeking to locate a trunk that had been washed away by the waters and asking the finder to keep the clothing it had contained but to return to the *Reveille* office any papers that might have survived.

In the same issue appeared this item:

HIS OCCUPATION GONE. — Sam, the Piute, who used to make a business of cleaning Main Street before the cloudburst came and smashed it all to smithereens, sits in the street on a boulder during the daytime, looking as blue as a Boston schoolmarm and gazing at the wreck, his occupation gone. Owing to his cleaning duties in previous years, Sam had been unable to attend the festivities of the pine-nut harvest, but this year he can join the throng of Indians to the mountains and "heap catchum pine-nut."

II

WITHIN a month, however, all reference to the flood had disappeared from its columns, and the paper, having boasted mildly of its new quarters and equipment, looked hopefully ahead, its confidence in the town's future and its own unimpaired by the disaster.

But it presently grew clear even to the *Reveille's* invincibly optimistic owners that Austin's first brief season of prosperity was destined also to be its last. For although there were occasional flurries of renewed activity as one mine or another struck pay ore and resumed operations until its ledges played out, these but served to emphasize that the town, and the area it served, were inexorably sinking back into insignificance.

With population growing less year by year and a slow

stagnation creeping over its business life, it was, of course, not long until the paper felt the blight of protracted hard times. The consequence was that the next two decades saw a succession of changes of ownership. In the fall of 1878, some three months after the disastrous flood, Fred Hart, during whose term as editor the *Reveille* had been widely known and frequently quoted all over the west, sold out his interest to his partner, John Booth, and left for greener fields.

Booth continued as owner and publisher until his death in the late 1880's, whereupon the property passed to his widow. Other changes followed. On January 28, 1889, Mrs. Booth sold the paper to G. A. Carpenter who had been managing its affairs since her husband's death. This arrangement, however, lasted only a few months, and on January 6, 1890, Carpenter announced that, having been unable to complete the purchase, the ownership was reverting to Mrs. Booth. A few weeks later, on June 30, the paper was again sold, this time to the Lander Publishing Company, and a veteran Nevada newspaperman, G. W. Rutherford, became editor; then, on July 18, the Lander Publishing Company sold out to two local residents, Hinchcliffe and Dennis — the latter an Austin attorney — with Rutherford continuing in the editorial post.

All this time the little paper had appeared six times a week. On November 11, 1890, however, came the announcement that, the town being no longer able to support a daily, the *Reveille* was resuming its original status as a weekly; thereafter, it would appear each Friday, with a new editor, A. H. Phillips, and a new, larger page-size. In that form it continued until January 25, 1893, when yet another change of ownership brought with it a return

to its original 11½ by 15½ inch format. At the same time,
Editor Phillips retired, ending twelve years' connection
with the journal.

The new proprietor and editor was W. D. Jones, who
for two years had been publishing a rival weekly in Austin, the *People's Advocate*. Upon purchasing the *Reveille*,
he combined the two and published it twice a week, on
Wednesdays and Saturdays. It presently grew clear, however, that the moldering town could not support a semiweekly, and the *Reveille* thereupon again became a
weekly.

It has so remained ever since. For despite shrinking cir-
culation and falling advertising revenue, the indestructi-
ble little journal has continued to hang on year after year.
During the first three decades of the present century,
there were frequent changes of ownership, and a succession of editors. Then, in 1933, the property came into pos-
session of a man who was to guide its destinies for the
next sixteen years. This was William M. Thatcher, a
seventy-year-old attorney who as a youth had edited his
father's newspaper in Lawrence, Kansas, and had since
had a picturesque career in many fields and places. His acquaintance with the Reese River country had begun in
1918, when the British owners of a mine in nearby Washington Canyon sent him out to superintend its development. He remained there four years, whereupon the backers, having tired of paying assessments and despairing
of ever getting any return on their investment, withdrew
their support.

Thatcher, however, still had faith in the property and six
years later returned as manager and work was resumed
under new owners. But this second attempt proved no

more successful than the first and after a few months the mine was again shut down, this time permanently.

Following this second disappointment, the elderly ex-lawyer and ex-miner, having meanwhile settled in Austin, decided to devote his declining years to the calling he had followed in his youth. Failing in an attempt to buy the *Reveille* from its then owner, one Doug Tandy, he early in 1933 founded a rival weekly, the *Austin Sun*, thus giving the decaying town's few remaining residents their choice of two local papers. However, this state of affairs lasted only a few months before Tandy, recognizing the obvious fact that the town could not support both, sold out to his competitor. Thatcher thereupon merged the *Sun* with the *Reveille* and assumed the editorial chair.

He continued to occupy that post until 1949, retiring then at the ripe age of eighty-seven. Throughout that period, the longest served by any of the paper's editors, he breathed new life into the little sheet, making it once more the recognized spokesman of a large segment of central Nevada, its vigorous editorial policy wielding influence and commanding respect throughout the state.

During the greater part of that time, the old editor literally "lived on the job." For shortly after he bought the paper, he became so crippled with rheumatism that he was unable to negotiate Austin's steep streets. Accordingly, he moved the paper into the small brick building it occupies today, fitted up living quarters in the back room, and made arrangements to have the printing done at the plant of the *Standard* at Fallon, a town some one hundred twenty miles to the west. Seated at his ancient roll-top desk, beside a window that looked out on the town's once-teeming but then almost deserted main street, he composed his sonorous editorials, championing every cause that might further the interests of the Reese River country and hasten the day when it would, as he firmly believed, resume its oldtime importance.

Following his death in 1954, at the age of ninety-one, an admiring friend thus described him:

Winter and summer he wore a hat to protect his head from drafts, and an old sheepskin-lined coat hung over the back of the chair. . . . He rolled his own cigarettes and fragments of tobacco and ash covered the litter of papers spread before him. He enjoyed hot chocolate, and used a giant cup to drink from . . . The snow-white whiskers frilling around his chin gave him an air of venerability. But there was nothing old about his bright blue eyes, alert and observant as the eyes of a man in the prime of life. Nor was there anything old about his mind, an open, inquiring, receptive mind that was never closed to new ideas, new thoughts, and new adventures.

In 1953, four years after his retirement, Thatcher, then living in Oakland, California, thus wrote his successor on the occasion of the *Reveille's* ninetieth birthday:

It is an unusual — perhaps a unique — situation when a town, a newspaper, and the man who for years was the editor of that newspaper, all reach their ninetieth anniversaries at the same time.

I am the senior of the three — some two months older than the paper and about a month older than the town — but we were all associated for so long that I believe people have begun to regard us as identical triplets. . . .

The comparison was an apt one, for in the minds of all who had any knowledge of central Nevada during that period, Austin, the *Reveille,* and its venerable editor were so closely associated that they were looked on as virtually indivisible. As regards the first two of that triumvirate — the town and the paper — the feeling that they were one and the same has been universally held by residents of the Reese River country for close to a century. And with reason. For the camp and its newspaper had their beginnings together, together grew and prospered during the few years of plenty, and then throughout the decades that followed, shared the long, slow decline that reduced both to their present status, Austin as a sleepy village, its single street dotted here and there with a few sagging relics of its gaudy past, and the *Reveille,* once an acknowledged leader among western journals, an obscure, but still lively and pugnacious, country weekly.

III

VISITORS to Austin today have difficulty picturing it as it was in its heyday. For where, three quarters of a century and longer ago, unbroken rows of brick and stone business structures lined its main street for a distance of more than a mile, now the highway sweeps up the canyon past a single, two-block-long huddle of weatherbeaten buildings, some occupied, the majority with their façades lacking doors and windows and their interiors a shambles of collapsed floors and partitions and fallen roof timbers.

When a place that was never large in the first place undergoes a slow but steady decline for the better part of a century, few visible evidences of its past importance are likely to remain. Of the closely built cottages and cabins that once covered the canyonsides, only a few scattered remnants remain, most of them unoccupied. For Austin's population has in recent years continued its decline, and at an accelerated rate. Austin Township, embracing the southern half of Lander County and having an area more than twice that of Rhode Island, had, at the time the last census was taken, a total population of four hundred nineteen, that being a loss of more than 25 per cent since 1940 when the figure stood at five hundred eighty.

Yet, like all once-active western mining towns, Austin has its group of old-timers, their number diminishing year by year, who stoutly maintain that the adjacent hills and canyons conceal ledges as rich as any uncovered in the high-rolling 1860's, and who look forward with confidence to the day when the chimneys of a score of mills will again send columns of smoke into the desert air above the Toiyabes. The faith of these ancients is shared to a degree by most other residents, though with the latter it is more a hope than a conviction. For both by background and training, most native Nevadans are intensely mineral-conscious, and this, of course, includes virtually all the Austinites.

Question one of them about the possibility of a revival and he is likely to reply about as follows: "Sure, the Austin mines are all played out — have been for years — and that goes for the whole Reese River country. Hasn't been a ton of worth-while ore found here in a coon's age. Doesn't take any experts to tell us we're all washed up. Yet, if you go back eighty or ninety years, you'll find that some of the richest ledges in the whole history of mining were found right here. Of course, they've all been scraped dry — all that were ever found, that is. But who can be sure there aren't others? Stands to reason, doesn't it, that there might still be some pretty likely claims hereabouts, waiting for somebody lucky enough to find them?"

For while the present-day resident views the future of his town with a healthy and well-founded skepticism, he doesn't write off entirely the possibility of a second major mining boom. The prevailing attitude seems to be that, granted that monumental piece of luck, the place can have a future to match its lusty past — and thus the faith of those who have stayed on during the intervening years would be triumphantly vindicated. It is only thus that the persistence of the town over the past half-century can be explained. On any other grounds it would be difficult to see why more than the veriest handful of people should have chosen to remain.

For when the area's first profitable ledges pinched out more than sixty years ago, the sole reason for the existence of a sizable town there vanished. Thereafter, Austin became, like a dozen other villages strung across the plains from Salt Lake to the Sierra, a way station on one of the overland highways, its primary function to provide food, shelter, and incidental supplies to transients.

To be sure, it serves, too, as a source of supplies for ranchers in the adjacent valleys, and for those working the few mining claims that are intermittently active in the area. Also, being the only town within a radius of forty miles, it is something of an educational center, drawing pupils to its high school from distant points throughout the region.

However, the number living within the district served by the town is so small that Austin's business life, limited as it is, could not maintain itself on their trade alone. It is, as stated, the patronage of the traveling public that keeps it from shrinking still further. For, in a small way, present-day Austin is a tourist center. This is not due to its historical importance, for few who pass through have any knowledge of its gaudy past, but merely to the fact that it chances to be located on two main-traveled highways.

The chief of these is U.S. 50, the old Lincoln Highway, which crosses Nevada east and west and has for more than a century witnessed an unbroken flow of through traffic; first the pathfinding hunters and trappers, then the slow-moving wagons of the California gold-seekers, the Pony Express riders, the transcontinental stages of pre-railroad days, and, after the turn of the century and continuing down to the present, the ever-lengthening caravans of automobile tourists.

To be sure, the greater part of the trans-state motor traffic no longer passes through Austin, for in recent years much of it swings farther north and follows U.S. 40, which closely parallels the route of the Southern Pacific Railroad through the Humboldt Valley. Nonetheless, a considerable number of motorists continue to take the historic central route, and their business, together with that of those traveling on State Highway 8-A, a recently improved north-south road, supports the town's few motels and filling stations and gives welcome trade to its hotel and restaurants and grocery stores.

It is, however, not on these factors alone that today's residents base their unshakable belief in the permanance of their town. For Austin, as they never fail to point out, has yet another anchor to windward, one that will sustain it in the future just as it has done for a period beyond the memory of the oldest inhabitant. They are referring, of course, to the fact that for more than ninety years Austin has been the seat of government for Lander County — and Lander County's far-flung borders embrace an area larger than that of several eastern states.

This is a mark of distinction to which the citizens point with pride. The town's chief architectural ornament, its sturdy, eighty-year-old courthouse, to them stands as a symbol of Austin's preeminence as the legislative, judicial, and administrative center of more than fifty-six hundred square miles of central Nevada. For here, at the county seat, are stationed those officials charged with conducting its affairs: the sheriff, the assessor and tax collector, and others; here, too, are the county jail and the county hospital, and the room where the county commissioners hold their monthly meetings and the superior judge periodically presides at sessions of the county court.

It is true that in playing this role, Austin has been beset with a number of complications. One long-standing problem has been that of filling certain county offices, notably those of the district attorney and the county health officer. The difficulty here is that both officials must be men of professional training — an attorney and a physician — and that, their official duties being relatively light, they are hired on a part-time basis and their salaries are fixed accordingly. The consequence is that these officers must augment their incomes by engaging in private practice, something that is hardly feasible in so small a village. This has resulted in a situation said to be unique in the entire country; that is, a county seat having so few inhabitants that two important county officials must live elsewhere in order to support themselves. For many years, the holders of these posts have maintained their homes and offices at Battle Mountain, at the opposite end of the county, making the ninety-mile trip to Austin whenever county business requires their presence there.

The citizens of Battle Mountain, the county's largest town — with a population of only a few hundred — have long maintained that their metropolis is better qualified to serve as the official headquarters of Lander County than tiny, isolated Austin. Accordingly, for more than three decades, campaigns have regularly been launched to have the county seat transferred to that point. These moves the Austin residents have fought tooth and nail, and thus far with success. Their chief argument, a potent one with the voters of the county, is that such a transfer would necessitate the building of a new courthouse in the northern town, a needless waste of the taxpayers' money since Austin's venerable but still sturdy brick building is not only quite adequate for the county's present needs but, with a bit of refurbishing and modernization, for many years in the future.

However, the long-drawn-out county seat battle is by no means over. That ·Austin is not yet ready to throw in the sponge became abundantly clear as recently as 1953. Early that year, a group of merchants in Battle Mountain reopened the prolonged battle by having petitions circulated among the voters of the county calling for a special election to decide whether or not the courthouse would be moved. When the required number of signatures were obtained and the election date duly fixed, the Battle

Mountain residents were jubilant, and apparently for good reason. For a clear majority of Lander County's one thousand eight hundred inhabitants lived in the north and — so it was argued — these, of course, would all favor the transfer.

But it soon grew clear that the Austinites had no intention of letting the election go by default. Their town had been Lander County's seat of government for more than nine decades and its residents promptly served notice that they were not going to permit it to be moved elsewhere — at least, not without a struggle. Accordingly, the citizens met in conclave, organized the Lander County Taxpayers Association, and prepared to wage vigorous counterwarfare. They did not fail to point out that, should the move be approved by the voters, the Lander County taxpayers would face the necessity of building a new county headquarters at Battle Mountain — a needless expense, since Austin's sturdy brick courthouse was quite adequate for the county's present and future needs.

When the northerners retorted that the ancient Austin structure — it was built in 1867 — was in so ramshackle a state that "from $75,000 to $80,000" would be required to put it in serviceable condition, the Austinites promptly branded the charge "pure poppycock." Moreover, they backed up their claim by hiring an expert, the building inspector of the city of Reno, to examine the structure and render an opinion. His report, duly publicized in the columns of the *Reveille,* stated that "the building is structurally sound in every respect; much more so than many public buildings erected today; and it is good for use for another 150 to 200 years."

From then on, the campaign waxed fast and furious,

with charges and countercharges being hurled weekly in the columns of the Austin and Battle Mountain papers. In this exchange the *Reveille*, true to its traditions as a fighting journal, more than held its own, its astute editor, Jock Taylor, heaping ridicule on each claim advanced by the northerners.

A story is being circulated in Battle Mountain [he wrote on May 30] to the effect that some Battle Mountain woman — unidentified, of course — narrowly escaped injury when a large portion of the plaster ceiling in one of the court house offices fell down and narrowly missed crushing her. As every ceiling in the court house is of matched boards — not plaster — there seems something wrong with that story. While it may have been possible that the Battle Mountain woman got plastered in Austin, she certainly didn't get plastered in the court house.

By way of answering Austin's contention that to move the county seat to the northern town would put Lander County taxpayers to heavy expense, the Battle Mountain adherents retorted that adequate quarters could be provided there at extremely moderate cost. Their statement that the county officers could function efficiently even if housed temporarily in a Quonset hut, brought this prompt rejoinder from the *Reveille's* editor:

As a matter of fact, there is no money to finance even a Quonset hut, so why waste time over that consideration? Why spend any money at all? Surely, there must be somewhere in Battle Mountain an old shed that could be used for the purpose, or even an unused and oversized public privy, which at least could quite aptly be called the county seat. Either would be as appropriate for the purpose as a Quonset hut. . . .

Meantime, the embattled Austinites were waging warfare on another front. Having engaged the services of a leading Reno attorney to represent its interests, the Lander County Taxpayers Association challenged the legality of the coming election before the county commissioners, contending that the petition did not contain the names of the required three fifths of the qualified voters. Despite this, however, two of the three commissioners, both from the north, signed an order authorizing the election and proceeded with the printing of the ballots.

The Austin group thereupon carried the matter into court and, in late July, obtained from the District Judge an injunction forbidding the holding of the election until the arguments pro and con could be heard. This decision the Battle Mountain faction promptly appealed to the State Supreme Court and, the date for the election being by then close indeed, that body agreed to hear the testimony the following Monday, September 15, and to render a decision that same day.

During the hearing, a perplexing legal point was brought out. The attorney for the Austin interests pointed out that by state law an election for the removal of a county seat must be held within sixty days after it had been authorized. Opposing counsel countered by citing another section of the statute which required that in such elections the close of registrations must be advertised for thirty days, and that another thirty days must elapse thereafter before the election could be held. In other words, one section of the law specified that such elections must take place within sixty days after they had been authorized, whereas another provided that they could not legally be held before a sixty-one-day period had transpired.

The State Supreme Court, after pondering this weighty problem and concluding that the laws governing such elections were legally inoperative as they then stood, handed down its decision: namely, that no election of the kind could be conducted until the state legislature had amended the existing laws. Accordingly, the injunction was sustained, the election called off, and the Austinites breathed a mighty sigh of relief. For at least another year or two — until the state's lawmakers got around to straightening out the legal tangle — their town would continue to be Lander County's seat of government.

Meantime, the residents, although they make it unmistakably clear that they have no wish to convert the place into what they scornfully term a "professional ghost town," have become increasingly aware of the benefits to be derived from making known to the public something of the region's gaudy past. Accordingly, led by the *Reveille,* the citizens early in 1953 launched a campaign to install street signs calling the attention of visitors to various spots where stirring events had taken place in the early days, and to raise funds for the restoration of such historic buildings as still remained.

The first of these buildings to receive attention was a little stone structure at the upper edge of town, built by Reuel Colt Gridley in the early 1860's to house his flourishing grocery store, and from which he, carrying his celebrated sack of flour, set off on the nationwide tour that raised many thousands of dollars for the Sanitary Fund during the Civil War. With money contributed by the townspeople themselves, plus donations sent in by former residents all over the west, the building was rehabilitated and today houses the Austin Historical Museum, in which are displayed photographs, documents, mining tools, and an assortment of other articles dating from the long-distant past.

Encouraged by the response to this first appeal, plans are under way to reconstruct several other sagging buildings which still stand here and there on the once-crowded main street — including the little brick structure that was for many years the home of the *Reveille*. But the citizens are adamant on one point: it is no part of their plan to convert the town into a museum of antiquities. It is Austin's future that interests them, not its past, and visitors are here warned that the one sure way to affront them is to refer to their little cluster of weatherbeaten buildings as a ghost town.

As a matter of fact it is well within the realm of possibility that Austin may some day — and in the not too distant future — become once more the teeming, bustling place it was during its brief heyday. While the likelihood of any substantial revival of its once booming silver-mining industry is admittedly a remote one, it now appears that the Reese River district may have yet other strings to its bow. For during the past year or two the whole area has been searched and re-searched for three no less valuable substances: namely, oil, tungsten, and uranium. Of these, the last-named now appears to offer the greatest promise. Throughout the summer of 1954 amateur and professional prospectors, each armed with his Geiger counter, poured into the region in such numbers that Austin's limited facilities for accommodation were taxed to — and beyond — their limits, while test borings were made on several newly located claims to determine if their uranium-bearing ores were of sufficient richness to warrant full-scale development. Should that prove to be the case, it could well be that Austin may yet stage its long anticipated comeback, and that "The Town That Died Laughing" will have the triumphant last laugh, this time at the expense of those who for a generation and more have been consigning it to oblivion.